DELIVERANCE
TO
FREEDOM

A GUIDE FOR RELEASING
CAPTIVES

REGINA SHANK

First Printing: 2017

ISBN: 978-1-9744-6042-7

Cover design by Amani Hanson (Becoming Studios, noboxez@yahoo.com).

Editing supervision, text design and typesetting by Jim Bryson (JamesLBryson@gmail.com).

Editing by Emilyanne Zornes (pcome.proofandcopy@gmail.com)

Contents

Foreword

There is currently a flurry of interest and activity in the ministry of deliverance and inner healing that arguably has not been seen since the Jesus movement of the 1970's. I believe the Lord is bringing this ministry back to the forefront.

Hosea 4:6 says, "My people perish, or are destroyed for lack of knowledge." The church has been wandering in the wilderness in this area of ministry for much too long. It's time to see the church take its rightful place and God's people set free.

As the presiding Apostle and President of the International Society of Deliverance Ministers, I get numerous requests to review books on the subject of deliverance and healing. Honestly, I'm very selective about which books I consider putting my name on. Regina Shank's book was one I am so delighted to have had the pleasure of reading and commenting on. I've personally known Regina for many years; she's the real deal! She has done a great service to the body of Christ by sharing real-life situations from her vast experiences acquired during her 25+ years in ministry!

Just scan the chapter titles in the Table of Contents and you'll be just as excited to read it as I was. Inside, you'll find not only practical teaching, but riveting true-life testimony of God's grace and delivering power. The final chapter: "Freedom Map, The Way Out," unpacks the weapons of our warfare, which are indeed mighty in God for the pulling down of strongholds.

I highly recommend this work and this co-laborer in the ministry of deliverance!

Blessings,
Dr. William (Bill) Sudduth
President ISDM & RAM Ministries

<u>Prelude</u>

What Does Freedom Look Like?

What does freedom look like? Is it the absence of conflict or problems? I don't think that's possible in this life. We live in a fallen world, a world that has lost its footing. Paradise was lost when the first man, Adam and Eve, relinquished their standing with God, and chose their own way. Mankind, designed to function in the Presence of God, designed to be led by the Spirit of God, lost access to God when disobedience brought separation from His Presence and disconnected us from His wisdom.

> *Now the Lord is the Spirit, and where the Spirit of the Lord is, there is liberty [emancipation from bondage, true freedom].*
>
> 2 Corinthians 3:17 AMP

True freedom is found in His Presence. Through Jesus, we regain access to our Heavenly Father. Jesus became the living sacrifice, paying for our sins with His blood laying down His life and becoming a bridge to cross over into the restoration of the relationship with God that we (mankind) lost at the fall.

In Acts 8, a man named Simon tried to purchase the ability to impart Holy Spirit to others. Peter rebuked him with these words, *"For I see that you are full of bitterness and captive to sin"* (Acts 8:23 NIV). The words spoken by Peter describe the opposite of freedom. Simon was in bondage to bitterness and incarcerated by the sin of a heart separated from God.

> *For everything in the world—the lust of the flesh,*
> *the lust of the eyes, and the pride of life—comes*
> *not from the Father but from the world.*
>
> 1 John 2:16 NIV

Yielding to the lust of the flesh, lust of the eyes, and the pride of life puts us on the road to bondage and captivity. But Jesus made it possible to be in the world, and not of the world.

> *If you belonged to the world, it would love you as*
> *its own. As it is, you do not belong to the world,*
> *but I have chosen you out of the world. That is*
> *why the world hates you.*
>
> John 15:19 NIV

Several years ago, while in prayer, I stepped into a vision where I was walking down a corridor of a prison. On either side of me were prison cells, each holding a person. It seemed endless. I noticed there were no doors on these cells, just bars that incarcerated the prisoners. That's when the Lord spoke to me:

"I want you to free them."

"There are no doors on these cells. How do I free them?" I said.

I will never forget the power of His next words; they resounded like thunder and shook the prison.

"I AM THE DOOR!!"

Suddenly, doors appeared in each cell and swung open toward me. I reached into one of the cells and pulled the person out. I then walked to the next cell to bring out another prisoner. One by one, they walked through the doors that had appeared when Jesus spoke those powerful words. I continued pulling them out. In one of the cells, I took hold of a person's arm but they refused to come. Fear of the unknown was too much for them. They chose the safety of the familiar prison rather than risking stepping into a freedom they had never experienced.

I was beginning to understand our Lord's commission from Isaiah (as recorded in Luke).

> *"The Spirit of the Lord is on me, because he has anointed me to proclaim good news to the poor. He has sent me to proclaim freedom for the prisoners and recovery of sight for the blind, to set the oppressed free, to proclaim the year of the Lord's favor."*
>
> Luke 4:18-19 NIV

Freedom is a choice. Yet, it is hidden from view until the eyes of hearts are enlightened to see the door.

> *So Jesus said again, "I assure you and most solemnly say to you, I am the Door for the sheep [leading to life]. All who came before Me [as false messiahs and self-appointed leaders] are thieves and robbers, but the [true] sheep did not hear*

them. I am the Door; anyone who enters through Me will be saved [and will live forever], and will go in and out [freely], and find pasture (spiritual security)."

John 10:7-9 AMP

The Lord has made a way to bring us fully out of our past to bring us fully into our future. Freedom is costly. It will cost you your bondages. You must face your fears and confront them with boldness, knowing the door is open and the price has been paid to set you free. Running from the pain of abuse, trauma, addiction, or rejection is not the answer. Numbing the pain with any physical source may give temporary respite, but only Jesus can uproot its source, and permanently dislodge its influence from your life.

I pray that you read this book in the power of Holy Spirit our deliverer, with Jesus our Great Physician. Together, let us find true liberty from oppression and fear by walking through the Door leading us out of our past, and stepping fully into our future.

Let the adventure begin.

Regina Shank

1

Overcomers

*"I have told you these things, so that in Me
you may have [perfect] peace. In the world you
have tribulation and distress and suffering, but
be courageous [be confident, be undaunted, be
filled with joy]; I have overcome the world. [My
conquest is accomplished, My victory abiding.]"*

John 16:33 AMP

It's true. We live in a fallen world; a seductive world. The sights,
sounds, smells, pictures, music, movies, sometimes even friends,
beckon us to enjoy illegitimate delicacies. The Lord created the
world for us to enjoy. He wants us to have abundant life, but within
the boundaries set by His love.

Within each of us is a desire to be loved, valued, and accepted.
We were born with a purpose we are destined to fulfill. One enemy
of that purpose is our flesh. Even as the world seeks to conquer
us by appealing to our carnal nature, the Lord provides a way of
escape from its grasp. One person conquered the world's seductive
power completely. The Son of God overcame, giving us hope that

through His spirit we too can overcome.

Partaking of illegitimate pleasures that destroy or delay the purpose for which we were created, gives a victory to the prince of this world. He is a roaring lion seeking someone to devour. Let's face it, there is pleasure in sin, but sin produces death. Another problem with sin is that it's illegitimate—which means it's outside the boundaries God has set for us, and opens a door of access to darkness.

> *"If you do what is right, will you not be accepted? But if you do not do what is right, sin is crouching at your door; it desires to have you, but you must rule over it."*

Genesis 4:7 NIV

Ruling over what's been sent to rule over you is a constant battle. But be encouraged, it gets easier. Because Jesus overcame the world and its lusts, we have power through Him to do the same.

The Bible tells us that His strength is made perfect in our weakness. Suppose you are being tempted with a wrong heart attitude such as jealousy. You feel disappointed, hurt, and discontent with your life. You have a friend who appears to have it all. You want what they have, don't have it, and so you're jealous and resentful toward them. The next step is to tear them down with your words. Your heart becomes full of jealousy, accusation, and bitterness toward them.

Several years ago, I was confronted by a person who felt rejected, jealous, and angry at me. I had no idea she felt that way. It was a Sunday morning—church was about to start—when this woman came up to me and said, "There isn't room in this church for both of us."

I was on my way to the rest room, so I dodged her and continued on my way. When I came out of the stall, there she was, waiting to confront me again. She began to speak, when another woman came through the door. I slipped out between them and returned to the sanctuary for the beginning of the service. After the service, I slipped out the side door and was able to avoid any contact with her. The rest of that week, I prayed for her asking God to heal her disappointed heart. I was scheduled to preach the next week. I can't remember what subject I presented, but I do remember asking those who needed ministry to come to the front. Several came forward. I moved down the line praying for each one for various needs. I moved to the next person and there she was, the woman I had avoided last week. Slipping out the side door at that moment would not have been appropriate. I had to face her. She looked at me and began to cry.

"You have it all." She blurted. "I have nothing. I know I have a call of God on my life, but there's no room for me here. You are in my way."

I reached out to her, put my arms around her, and allowed her to weep on my shoulder. As the tears flowed, the disappointment surfaced, and the vulnerability of the moment allowed entrance for the Spirit's touch. I was able to speak to her.

"You don't want what I have. You want what the Lord has for you. He loves you and is faithful to prepare you for what He has prepared for you. Let Him heal you of your disappointment. Allow Him to fill your heart with His love to the point that you can rejoice over the success of others. There is plenty of room in God's Kingdom for all of us, and He is not withholding from you. He has a timing for each of us to be fully released. What He has prepared for you is worth the wait."

She lifted her eyes, looked me in the face, and said, "I'm sorry. Please forgive me for jealousy and resentment toward you."

In that moment, she took a giant leap forward. Her flesh had become jealous, but she conquered it. She realized the jealousy was delaying the fulfillment of what God had for her. She followed the Biblical directive to:

> *Confess your faults one to another, and pray one for another, that ye may be healed. The effectual fervent prayer of a righteous man availeth much.*

James 5:16 KJV

She also realized she could not illegitimately take an anointing from another person; it had to come from the Lord Himself to her.

She continued to demonstrate humility, and eventually, the Lord released her into an Intercessory ministry that she continues to this day. What was sent to overcome her, she overcame through humility and dependence on the strength of the Lord.

> *For all that is in the world—the lust and sensual craving of the flesh and the lust and longing of the eyes and the boastful pride of life [pretentious confidence in one's resources or in the stability of earthly things]—these do not come from the Father, but are from the world.*

I John 2:16 AMP

I've often described the flesh as a two-year-old child, pounding on his highchair tray, demanding his way, throwing food at mom, kicking his feet, and having a major tantrum. Without the overcoming power of Jesus, we too will want what we want, when we want it, and demand that life give us the cravings of our flesh.

In physics, we learn that there is matter and anti-matter. A couple of examples are the electron and the positron, the proton and the neutron.

> *A positron is a particle of matter with the same mass as an electron but an opposite charge. It is a form of anti-matter because, when a positron encounters an electron, the two completely annihilate to yield energy. The existence of the positron was predicted in 1928 by physicist Paul Dirac, and positrons were discovered experimentally in 1932 by Carl Anderson*
>
> whatis.techtarget.com/definition/positron

The positron is not the only known anti-matter particle. The proton and the neutron have antiparticles as well, known as the anti-proton and the anti-neutron, with negative and neutral electrical charges, respectively.

The clash between these positives and negatives, matter and anti-matter, causes them to annihilate each other. Even from physics, we learn that the world is a hostile place. When a proton exists in a vacuum, it does not encounter the anti-proton. I liken this to being in the world, but not of the world. Jesus said in the world we will have tribulation, trials, and opposition to the abundant life He chose for us. The enemy of our souls, Satan, is the opposing force released in the fallen world whose goal is to annihilate us. The Bible says,

The thief comes only to steal and kill and destroy;
I have come that they may have life, and have it
to the full.

John 10:10 NIV

So being in the world but not of the world, is key to avoiding destructive forces arrayed against us. In the wilderness for forty days and nights, Jesus encountered the destructive force of Satan himself. In one of those temptations, Jesus was offered the kingdoms of the world if He would only bow down and worship the adversary.

Again, the devil took him to a very high mountain
and showed him all the kingdoms of the world
and their splendor. "All this I will give you," he
said, "if you will bow down and worship me."
Jesus said to him, "Away from me, Satan! For it is
written: 'Worship the Lord your God, and serve
him only."

Matthew 4:8-10 NIV

This is the lie presented to each of us by the enemy of our soul. Even as he tried to seduce Jesus into worshipping him by offering Him the kingdoms of this world, he will also tempt us with the same deception. Those kingdoms were his because of the fall. He could give them, but destruction would inevitably follow. The world has the power to draw us in. It's called the lust of the eyes, the lust of the flesh, and the pride of life. Jesus turned down Satan's offer, using the word of God to defeat His adversary. He trusted the power of His Father's word and stood firmly on it instead of falling for temporary deceptive gain.

Overcomers

The works of the flesh are listed in Galatians:

> *The acts of the flesh are obvious: sexual immorality, impurity and debauchery; idolatry and witchcraft; hatred, discord, jealousy, fits of rage, selfish ambition, dissensions, factions and envy; drunkenness, orgies, and the like. I warn you, as I did before, that those who live like this will not inherit the kingdom of God.*
>
> Galatians 5:19-21

One of the works of the flesh listed is witchcraft. A young girl was playing around with it. She thought it would help her control her world, and it promised to do so. She cast spells on people, attended a few witch gatherings, bought a book on witchcraft and opened a door to darkness. One night she was laying in her bed when Satan appeared and told her she belonged to him now. It scared her so badly that she called a friend and asked her what to do. The friend told her to get out of witchcraft—that it wasn't a game. It was real and she was actually playing with darkness. I happened to be mentoring the friend who was advising her. Her friend told her to call me. She came in the next day and poured out her story.

She gave her heart and life to Jesus, renounced Satan, and broke all ties to darkness. She is still in my Prophetic Mentoring class and has a revelatory gift that she uses to encourage others. Because she was hungry for the supernatural and didn't see it in any churches she attended, she turned to witchcraft. She encountered the spiritual realm through an illegitimate door. But that door is now shut through repentance, and she has opened the door to legitimate spiritual knowledge based on the word of God through a relationship with Jesus.

Dissension is another work of the flesh. Have you ever met people who love to argue? Not only that, but they tend to carry bits of juicy information from one person to another with the intention of stirring up a pot of strife. They stir it occasionally, keeping the fire going and emotions boiling. Living the life of a soap opera character, their drama swells and recedes like the tide of an ocean. These people are to be avoided, but when they show up at work or school, in your family, or in your church, what do you do? First of all, pray for them. Then, refuse to be a player in the drama they create.

I had an encounter with such a person. She came into my facility and asked if she could speak to me privately and, instinctively, I knew it wasn't going to be good. She had to tell me her side of a story and wanted to know whose side I was on. I knew I had to guard my heart and avoid being pulled into any contention.

I thought to myself, "I'm not in this drama, and won't be pulled into it." I asked the Lord to show me the way of escape as she continued.

When she took a breath, I spoke quietly and firmly to her. "I am not involved in this situation. I knew little about it until you came trying to involve me. I have no desire to voice an opinion about it, and will not become a player in this drama. Perhaps, the best thing for you to do is to let go of your offense in this matter, and pray for everyone involved."

I gently asked the Lord to heal her heart and mend the situation. She stood up, left my office, and I haven't seen her since.

People who live by their flesh, rather than by the Spirit of

Overcomers

God, try to draw others into participating in their fleshly exploits. Conquering contention, witchcraft, jealousy, or any other work of the flesh is possible through the power of Jesus Christ, who told us to "take up our cross and follow Him." His flesh was crucified on a cross. We overcome when we allow His spirit to show us the way of escape from the world. As children of God, we learn to walk in His ways, and reject the ways of the world.

> *I have given them your word and the world has hated them, for they are not of the world any more than I am of the world. My prayer is not that you take them out of the world but that you protect them from the evil one. They are not of the world, even as I am not of it.*

> John 17:14-16 NIV

Deliverance To Freedom

2

Deliverance to Freedom

So do not fear, for I am with you; do not be dismayed, for I am your God. I will strengthen you and help you; I will uphold you with my righteous right hand.

Isaiah 41:10 NIV

I know how it feels to be rooted in rejection, abandonment, and fear. I was so rooted that I rarely spoke for fear it would come out wrong. Rejection had me in its grip. I could be in a crowded room and still feel alone. My emotions were scarred by adverse circumstances that marred my soul and marked my path. I was a rejected human being, so that's how I viewed life, through the lens of nonacceptance.

Overcoming rejection can become a primary goal in life sending one down a path of performance and competition or down the road to nowhere, where isolation from a painful life can become a lifestyle. Self-rejection can ultimately lead to suicide. Acceptance is a basic human need. When that need is not met, one can go to great lengths to find it or just give up altogether. I tried to win acceptance through performance. It wasn't that I wanted to make others look bad; I thought I had to excel at something to demonstrate value. It became a race with no finish line.

My journey through rejection has given me an awareness of the struggle in others. Some hide behind a façade of shallow smiles or shrill greetings. Some walk through a crowd showing off expensive clothes and sparkling diamonds. Or lurk in a corner trying to fade into nothingness. It can leave a trail of failed marriages and abandoned children. It can sing the loudest and show off its best only to feel alone after the party is over.

I remember the day my party was over. The loneliness and rejection became more than I could bear. I had known Jesus most of my life—as my friend, Savior, and King—but there were areas of my life I had not allowed Him to enter. How do you open the door to a place you sealed off years ago? And why would Jesus want to come into that place? I didn't even want to go there myself.

One day when I was sitting before the Lord, I heard these words in my Spirit, "You are going to have to turn around and face that three-legged dog."

I remembered when I was a little girl, probably three or four years old. I was playing in the yard, when a three-legged dog bounded toward me. I was terrified of it. An adult who was there yelled, "You better run! That dog is going to get you. Hurry! Hurry! Run!" I ran screaming in fear. That was a defining event in my life. The Lord showed me from that moment on, I had been running from my fears.

That dog represented the fears I wouldn't face. I knew my running had to stop. The Lord was speaking to me personally—it was time to open up the sealed door. A scripture came up in my spirit:

This is what the Sovereign LORD, the Holy One of Israel, says: "In repentance and rest is your salvation, in quietness and trust is your strength, but you would have none of it. You said, 'No, we will flee on horses.' Therefore you will flee! You said, 'We will ride off on swift horses.' Therefore your pursuers will be swift! A thousand will flee at the threat of one; at the threat of five you will all flee away, till you are left like a flagstaff on a mountaintop, like a banner on a hill." Yet the LORD longs to be gracious to you; therefore he will rise up to show you compassion. For the LORD is a God of justice. Blessed are all who wait for him!

Isaiah 30:15-18 NIV

THE CAVE

In prayer, I repented of running from my fears. I gave the Lord permission to open my heart to His healing. Suddenly, in a vision, I saw it—a deep dark cave filled with nothingness. I knew it was the empty space in my heart where love had never entered. There were gray stone walls, dim light, and cold air brought shivers to my skin. There was no place to rest, no reprieve, only gray hard stone, that created an empty cavern of extreme loneliness. In the darkest corner, purulent drainage from a wound had etched its path into the stone floor. Because I had sealed off its entrance, there was no way out of the nothingness, the loneliness, the isolation. Such a place screamed silently for help.

"Lord, You don't want to come here. It hurts too much to share the pain with anyone, especially You. This is no place for You."

"Child, invite me into your cave. I want to come in," He said.

At that moment, I remembered this scripture:

> *Here I am! I stand at the door and knock. If anyone hears my voice and opens the door, I will come in and eat with that person, and they with me.*

> Revelation 3:20 NIV

I whispered the word, "Come!" And He was there.

The cave filled with light. A stone table appeared laden with food. His Presence filled my cave, and suddenly its stone walls disappeared, its coldness vanished, the darkness fled at the entrance of His light. Jesus and I sat down at the table and began to eat. There was healing in that food, hope enveloped me, and the wound in the stone floor became a clear sparkling stream of pure water. Even now, when I remember the miraculous transformation I experienced in His Presence, I weep at His goodness toward me. He is the healer. The love and acceptance I longed for, I found in Him. I still remember that cave, but it's no longer dark, damp, or lonely. The Lord changed it with His healing love.

The enemy intended to trap me in a grip of pain and trauma that disallowed the destiny designed for me. But the life of God brought transforming power to break out, so I could conquer what was meant to destroy me. I find it difficult to adequately describe the power of transforming moments in His Presence. Yet, I know from experience, they are real.

Breaking out of rejection, abandonment, and fear is possible for anyone who is willing to face the pain, allowing the Lord to open up the wound, and pour His love into it. First, realize it's possible. Then willingly allow the Lord to open the eyes of your heart to see beyond the emotional pain. One of the tactics of the enemy is to isolate us from God and people. Pride tells us we have to hide our shame and pain, so others don't see how needy we are. Romans 3:23 tells us, *"For all have sinned and fall short of the glory of God."* Yet the Father, by His spirit, longs to free us from our sin, pain, and shame. Freedom comes through relationship with Him. Find that quiet place of prayer, pour out your heart to Him, allow His transforming love to enter the dark places of your soul.

> *Here I am, Lord. I confess that I have run from You instead of running to You. Forgive me for not trusting You with my pain and trauma. I know You are knocking on the door of my lonely cave. I open that door to You today. Wash me, heal me, fill my emptiness with Your perfect love. Open the eyes of my heart to see that Your love is greater than the rejection I have experienced. Touch every wound. I invite You into every trauma, knowing You can remove its power so it no longer dominates my life. I chose to sit under the waterfall of Your love. Come, Lord, Jesus.*

Fear, the Enemy of Love

> *But as for me, I will sing about your power. Each morning I will sing with joy about your unfailing love. For you have been my refuge, a place of safety when I am in distress. O my Strength, to you I sing praises, for you, O God, are my refuge,*

the God who shows me unfailing love.

Psalms 59:16-17 NLT

Fear is marketable. Hollywood packages it in drama and horror movies. People buy tickets to see it or rent movies to bring it home. And we don't even need to buy the packaged kind of fear, we encounter it in the news and sound bites—clips of war, violence, car wrecks, and tragedy. Preachers rail against it admonishing us to "Have faith in God!" as a remedy for fear. But faith isn't the remedy, love is. *"There is no fear in love; but perfect love casts out fear..."* (1 John 4:18).

Fear is a commodity, but it is also an enemy. It stands as a paper tiger in front of us threatening harm. It blocks our path and limits our movements to a small, safe, controlled area. I have known people who wouldn't leave their house because of fear. The seeds of fear planted in us by a fallen world, and the god of this world, Satan, can produce an invasive thorn bush of anxiety that must be removed by uprooting it. That thorn bush produces the poison fruit of panic. Wikipedia tells us this about Panic:

> *"The word derives from antiquity and is a tribute to the ancient god, Pan. One of the many gods in the mythology of ancient Greece: Pan was the god of shepherds and of woods and pastures. The Greeks believed that he often wandered peacefully through the woods, playing a pipe, but when accidentally awakened from his noontime nap he could give a great shout that would cause flocks to stampede. From this aspect of Pan's nature, Greek authors derived the word panikon, sudden fear,*

the ultimate source of the English word: panic."

https://en.m.wikipedia.org/wiki/Panic

A few years ago, I took a team to Israel. We felt the Lord had directed us to go to a source of the Jordan River and pray for the light of the gospel of Jesus Christ to flow from the source through that nation. The area is called Banias. When we reached the source of the Banias River, a main tributary of the Jordan, the team covered me in prayer and I released floating lit candles into the spring—declaring that Jesus, the Light of the world, would be the source of life in Israel. I did not see it, but the god, Pan, in his cave, appeared in front of one of our team members.

When we got back to the hotel, we had a team meeting to process what had just happened. After doing some research, we discovered the history of Banias. This is what we found:

> *Banias is the Arabic and modern Hebrew name of an ancient site that developed around a spring once associated with the Greek god Pan. Archaeologists uncovered a shrine dedicated to Pan and related deities, and the remains of an ancient city founded sometime after the conquest by Alexander the Great.*
>
> *The first mention of the ancient city during the Hellenistic period was in the context of the Battle of Panium, fought around 200-198 BCE, when the name of the place was given as Panion. Later the region was called Paneas (Greek: Π). Both names were derived from that of Pan, the god of the wild and companion of the nymphs."*

https://en.m.wikipedia.org/wiki/Banias

We had stepped into territory occupied by the demonic spirit called Pan. *"For God has not given us a spirit of fear, but of power and of love and of a sound mind"* (II Timothy 1:7 NKJV). The Word of God declares that fear is a spirit. We prayed for each team member, freeing them from any oppression or sickness caused by the demonic encounter. God's love and power brought deliverance, and we were able to finish our assignments in Israel.

The love of God is the remedy for fear and panic. The blood of the Lamb of God keeps us safe from the attacks of fear. But for complete deliverance, we must be uprooted from the soil of fear and transplanted into the soil of His love,

> *...that Christ may dwell in your hearts through faith; that you, being rooted and grounded in love, may be able to comprehend with all the saints what is the width and length and depth and height—to know the love of Christ which passes knowledge; that you may be filled with all the fullness of God.*

> Ephesians 3:17-19 NKJV

The demonic realm is real, but the love of God overpowers and nullifies the power of darkness. As the love of God washes out fear, we are transformed from fearful, intimidated, victimized persons to bold, love-filled, victorious children of God. The goal of fear is to keep us caged, but the love of God beckons us to break out of fear's grip and step into the adventure of a life lived to the fullest.

> *Father, I ask You to remove the thorn bush of fear from my life. Uproot it from my heart and soul. Forgive me for unknowingly opening the door to*

fear. Wash my mind of those openings. Fill me with Your perfect love that casts out fear. I know this will be a process, but I yield to it, knowing You are able to complete the work You have begun in me. Amen

Deliverance To Freedom

3

Speaking Truth to a Deceitful Heart

Blessed are the pure in heart, for they will see God

Matthew 5:8 NIV

The heart is deceitful above all things and it is extremely sick; Who can understand it fully and know its secret motives?

Jeremiah 17:9 AMP

If our own heart lies to us, which the above scripture indicates, how do we navigate a world that is also deceptive. False religions abound. Advertisers exaggerate. Even close friends and distant relatives can believe and propagate deceptive information. I don't like being deceived. I especially don't like it when it is intentional. Intentional deceivers use their power to manipulate others. Jesus called Satan the Father of lies—the ultimate deceiver.

He was a murderer from the beginning, not holding to the truth, for there is no truth in him.

Deliverance To Freedom

When he lies, he speaks his native language, for he is a liar and the father of lies

John 8:44 NIV

So, we have a combination of the ultimate deceiver out to kill us and a deceptive heart steering us in the wrong direction...and we end up with trouble right here in River City. Lies come in many forms but the intent is the same—to deceive! And lies can become so embedded in the heart, that they can even be perceived as truth.

Truth is not what you believe. It is not a precept, a concept, or a news broadcast. It is not a set of dogmatic rules to live by, nor is it discovered in a library filled with books. Truth is a person! Jesus said in John 14:6 NIV, *"I am the way and the truth and the life. No one comes to the Father except through me."*

Years ago, I found myself in a situation surrounded by people who all believed the same lies. When our children were little, we attended a small church that seemed friendly and inviting. I needed love and acceptance—they provided it. We enjoyed the relationships we developed in that small church environment with fellowship suppers, game nights, and family picnics. But all the while, there was a queasy feeling in the pit of my stomach. The Sunday morning teaching was dry and boring. There was no life in it. I was not allowed to take communion because they claimed I had not been baptized by one who had authority. They believed they were the only ones who had authority from God to baptize.

I knew Jesus. I had accepted Him as my Savior when I was a little girl. My sister and I loved to read the Bible and pray together. We attended church camp where we heard the truth about a loving God who loved us enough to die for our sins. We also went to a Bible-believing church where we were taught to read the Bible for ourselves and memorize scripture. Jesus was my friend and still is. So, the confusing claims and dry sermons that I heard on Sunday morning in that friendly, deceived, little church didn't ring true to me. I was told I had to follow multitudes of rules before Jesus would accept me.

In a Sunday evening class, I raised my hand to ask a question. "How do you know when or if you have followed enough rules to get to heaven?" The man who was teaching answered my question with this statement, "You won't know until you die and face God."

At home, I talked to Jesus about what I was hearing. I asked Him about the dichotomy of what I knew in my heart compared to the heavy requirements I was being inundated with. "Lord, I don't understand what they are talking about. It doesn't feel right to me. Please show me the truth. I don't want to be deceived. They have so many rules. I have to attend all their services, get baptized by them, and all because only *their* authority is valid. I'm so confused. Help me!"

I love the faithfulness of God! During this season, I was attending a local university working on a bachelor's degree. On a Tuesday morning, as I was driving to class, I continued to talk to God about my dilemma. Conflicting scriptures came to mind:

> *For it is by grace you have been saved, through faith—and this is not from yourselves, it is the gift of God, not as a result of works, so that no one may boast.*
>
> Ephesians 2:8-9 NIV

Therefore, my dear friends, as you have always

obeyed—not only in my presence, but now much more in my absence—continue to work out your salvation with fear and trembling.

Philippians 2:12 NIV

I cried out, "Lord, You have to speak to me in a big way. I'm not getting it. I don't want to be deceived. Is it works or grace? I need Your help. I'm surrounded by people who all say the same thing, that I have to obey a bunch of rules, and that's the way I grew up too. But it doesn't feel right. The rules change and then I'm in trouble. Surely, You aren't an abusive Father, who requires more of me than I'm equipped to give. I thought Jesus bought me and gave me the gift of salvation. When I think about Your grace, I feel a refreshing wind in my heart. When I think about following all the rules, it feels like a heavy yoke of bondage. Please speak to me in a big way. I need Your help, God. Is it works or grace? "

Just as I finished my prayer, a huge semi-truck drove by me with the word, GRACE, printed on the side of the trailer. You can't tell me that wasn't God. The timing was too perfect. The answer too concise...and it changed my life forever. Wow! What a God we serve!

I love my Jesus. He lived a sinless life because He knew I was incapable of doing so. He worked the works, so I could do the greater works of loving people, seeing them freed, healed and delivered from the darkness of deception, sin, and shame. He speaks to us when we cry out to Him desperately seeking answers. Hannah's words of rejoicing when she received her answer from God express my heart.

Then Hannah prayed and said: "My heart rejoices

in the LORD; in the LORD my horn is lifted high.
My mouth boasts over my enemies, for I delight
in your deliverance. There is no one holy like the
LORD; there is no one besides you; there is no
Rock like our God."

1 Samuel 2:1-2 NIV

We left the small, friendly church by standing firm on the rock of revealed truth. When we spoke to the leaders about taking our names off their roles, God gave me the strength to show them what He had shown me about putting people back under the law. I heard myself talking to them about the Tower of Babel, where men thought they could reach God, and how that was impossible, *"For all have sinned and fallen short of the glory of God"* (Romans 3:23). But when we finished talking, and I had shown them so many scriptures about God's grace that they had begun to see it, they refused to leave their traditions.

We found our way to a grace-believing, Spirit-led church that surrounded us with encouragement, prayers, and truth. We knew our names were written in the Book of Life, but after this close encounter with deception, I asked the Lord how to avoid that bondage ever again. Here are the keys He gave me.

1. Know the word of God and the God of the word. Read it for yourself. Don't just take someone's word for it. Be like the Bereans who searched the scriptures to confirm what they were being taught.

Now the Berean Jews were of more noble character
than those in Thessalonica, for they received the
message with great eagerness and examined the

Scriptures every day to see if what Paul said was true.

Acts 17:11 NIV

2. Make the Spirit of Truth your friend. His job is to reveal the things of the Father. He takes things not known and makes them known. He also opens up deeper understanding of the word of Truth. Reading the word, without the Spirit of Truth, is like skipping a rock on the surface of a lake. Allow Holy Spirit to take you deep sea diving.

> *But when He, the Spirit of truth, comes, He will guide you into all the truth; for He will not speak on His own initiative, but whatever He hears, He will speak; and He will disclose to you what is to come. He will glorify Me, for He will take of Mine and will disclose it to you. All things that the Father has are Mine; therefore I said that He takes of Mine and will disclose it to you.*

John 16:13-15

3. Remain teachable. How much of all knowledge do you possess? This is not a rhetorical question, but one worth pondering. Because we are limited in our understanding, a multitude of counselors provides safety. Listen to revelatory teaching from others who know God better than you do.

> *Where there is no [wise, intelligent] guidance, the people fall [and go off course like a ship without a helm], But in the abundance of [wise and godly] counselors there is victory.*

4. Ask Jesus for a hungry heart. A seeking heart will search out a matter using the standard of truth found in God's Word as the measurement for receptivity to what's being taught. The following scripture speaks of the *glory of kings*. A king rules over a domain. The first domain we are called to rule over is our own heart. Ask the Lord to show you the lies you believe. You will be surprised at how many there are. But knowing the truth brings freedom.

> *"It is the glory of God to conceal a matter, But the glory of kings is to search out a matter."*

Proverbs 25:2 AMP

5. Know that truth is a Person. Jesus was standing before Pilate when He was asked, "What is truth?" Jesus did not reply and I believe that's because Truth was standing right in front of him. No answer was necessary. Truth was staring him in the face. Tradition is a good thing, but revelation is a God thing. Do not allow your traditions to nullify the Word of God.

> *"Pilate therefore said to Him, "Are You are a king then?" Jesus answered, "You say rightly that I am a king. For this cause I was born, and for this cause I have come into the world, that I should bear witness to the truth. Everyone who is of the truth hears My voice." Pilate said to Him, "What is truth?" And when he had said this, he went out again to the Jews and said to them, "I find no fault in Him at all."*

John 18:37-38 NKJV

Deliverance To Freedom

> *So justice is driven back, and righteousness stands at a distance; truth has stumbled in the streets, honesty cannot enter. Truth is nowhere to be found, and whoever shuns evil becomes a prey. The LORD looked and was displeased that there was no justice.*

> Isaiah 59:14-15 NIV

I remember watching Superman when I was a little girl. I loved the catch-phrase they used to describe him, "Fighting for truth, justice, and the American way." But when I grew up to work with people, I began to recognize the lack of a standard of truth. Many live in a "feel good" world making choices from that standard instead of the Word of God. I'm not Superman or Wonder Woman, but I am fighting for truth.

For several years now, I've had a recurring dream. In it, I'm part of an army trying to take ground. It's an ancient battle fought with ancient weapons on horseback. We are dressed in armor, carrying large swords with which to strike our enemy. Suddenly the flag, or standard, falls to the ground. The standard bearer, whose job it was to carry it, has fallen wounded and dying. There is great confusion as the army has no standard to follow. I rush to pull the flag out of the dirt, lift it high for the troops to see, and ride toward the hill we are destined to take. The troops follow and we win the battle.

I believe we are in that battle right now. Truth has fallen in the streets. Someone has to recognize the need to lift it up, step to the front line and raise it up for all to see.

A heart full of truth is a heart without deceptive motives,

manipulative ways, or devious methods. Purity of heart starts with desire for change, and a love for the truth, even if it's costly. Truth is costly-it will cost you all of your deceptions! Matthew 5:8 NIV says, _"Blessed are the pure in heart, for they will see God."_

> _Father, in the name of Jesus, I give you permission to expose the deceptions of my heart. I desire to know the Truth and by the truth to be set free. Help me discern truth from lies. Give me a hunger for the Word of Truth. I chose to make the Spirit of Truth my friend. I trust Him to keep me on the path of life._
>
> _Let the words of my mouth and the meditation of my heart Be acceptable in Your sight, O LORD, my rock and my Redeemer._
>
> Psalms 19:14

Deliverance To Freedom

4

Retrieving Lost Dreams

Hope deferred makes the heart sick, but desire fulfilled is a tree of life.

Proverbs 13:12

Yesterday's dreams become tomorrow's disappointments... unless those expectations become reality. We were born to dream. Dreams are the motivation to move forward, to be creative, to move out of our comfort zone into the realm of possibilities. Losing one's dreams shuts the door on hope. Living one day at a time keeps the eyes of the heart fixed on today, but there are distant horizons beckoning us, promising adventure, joy, and fulfilled destiny. I believe every person has a purpose to fulfill. Psalms 139:16 NIV speaks of a book written for each of us, *"Your eyes saw my unformed body; all the days ordained for me were written in your book before one of them came to be."* That purpose, written in His book for us, is found in Jesus Christ.

Recently, I was speaking about hope and how important it is for forward movement. I described hope deferred, a condition that keeps us stuck in disappointment, unable to believe God for His promises. I noticed a woman standing in the back of the room, becoming more agitated until she slipped out the back door. After the gathering was over, I saw her re-enter the building and I felt the Spirit's prompting to talk with her. After I introduced myself, I told her I had noticed she slipped out the back door while I was talking. I asked, "Are you OK?"

"No, I'm not," she replied. "Don't talk to me about hope and dreams. I'm tired of hoping. It never happens! And it hurts every time I hear you happy people tell your breakthrough stories. I don't have any stories like that, just disappointment after disappointment." She began to cry. Dreaming was too painful for her disappointed heart. I was talking to someone who had lost hope and had relegated her dreams to a distant memory. She and I eventually developed a friendship, and she allowed the Lord to heal her heart of hope deferred. Her unfulfilled desires had created a blockage that only Jesus could remove.

Dreams are unfulfilled desires—even when the dream comes from God.

> "...but a son who is your own flesh and blood will
> be your heir." He took him outside and said, "Look
> up at the sky and count the stars—if indeed you
> can count them." Then he said to him, "So shall
> your offspring be."
>
> Genesis 15:4-5 NIV

Abram had his promise—his dream—given to him by God. We can, like Abram, try to fulfill the dream ourselves and create a counterfeit of our book. The promise of a son was delayed so many years it became impossible by natural means. They decided to help

God's idea out with a good idea, creating a child by Sarah's servant, Hagar. This, in turn, caused major problems for all of them. As soon as Hagar conceived, contention hit the household, Hagar fled into the desert to escape the conflict, and an angel had to speak to Hagar there in the desert wilderness:

"You are now pregnant and you will give birth to a son. You shall name him Ishmael, for the LORD has heard of your misery. He will be a wild donkey of a man; his hand will be against everyone and everyone's hand against him, and he will live in hostility toward all his brothers."

Genesis 16:11-12 NIV

Abram, Sarah, and Hagar learned that helping God out with a *good* idea was not a *God* idea. The good ideas conceived can actually delay or hinder the dreams God has for us. Many people make decisions about life using the "good or bad" measurement. This seems logical, but actually, it shuts down God's freedom to fulfill His dream. There were two trees in the Garden of Eden. The tree of the knowledge of good and evil was forbidden fruit. The other tree was the tree of life.

In my journey with God, the season came for me to learn to follow God's dreams instead of asking "Is this good or bad?" I learned to ask, "Does God want this?" I remember the day the Lord asked me to let Him lead.

It was a pretty normal day. I was driving along, thinking about the plans I had made to gather people together for a training seminar. I had put the pieces together, planned the curriculum, printed the flyer, invited the participants. It was a good idea.

Deliverance To Freedom

Suddenly, I heard the Lord speak to me with this question, "When are you going to quit building a stage for Me to perform on? Who is the Lord and who is the servant in this relationship?"

"Lord, what do You mean? I'm just wanting to give them more of You. I thought that's what You wanted me to do," I replied.

He spoke again, "From now on, I want you to lay down your good ideas, and come to me for direction and instruction. You are out of my timing. You are giving me direction instead of allowing me to direct you."

I immediately repented of my ignorance of His ways.

"Father, forgive me. I did not know what I was doing. Teach me. I really want to do it Your way."

In the days that followed, the eyes of my heart were opened to the necessity of being led by His Spirit. One day I ran into this scripture: *"For those who are led by the Spirit of God are the children of God"* (Romans 8:14 NIV). My life changed. My perception changed, and I realized I was not alone in a fallen world. I had a Father, who wanted to direct my feet into the path of life. He wanted me to have fulfilled dreams, to walk out the purpose He had for me in the earth. My self-effort was getting me nowhere. Another scripture had life-giving direction for me. *"But seek first his kingdom and his righteousness, and all these things will be given to you as well"* (Matthew 6:33 NIV)

Instead of seeking fulfillment of my dreams, my book of destiny, this scripture instructed me to seek Him and He would add the fulfillment to my life.

I've had hope deferred. I've been disappointed. Much of it was my lack of understanding of the ways of God. Without the wisdom, direction, timing, and revelation of God, we can wander and wonder, even blaming God for our false moves. I understand the pain of disappointment, the longing for the abundant life promised to us in John 10:10 , *"The thief comes only to steal and kill and destroy; I came that they may have life, and have it abundantly."* I've prayed with many people who have lost hope. As they gave the Lord access to the painful losses and disappointments, He performed heart surgery, restored the life flow, and brought drastic change to their lives. Dreams came alive again and circumstances began to line up for dreams to become a reality. Here is a prayer for dealing with hope deferred:

Lord, my heart is hurting. I long to see the fulfillment of the dreams you placed in my heart. I lay down my desires for yours. You said to delight myself in you, and you would give me the desires of my heart. Make your desires my desires. I give you the disappointments, the pain, the loss. Forgive me for blaming you for my missteps, my wrong motives, and my good ideas that have interfered with your plans for me. Heal my heart. Fill me with your love that removes the fear of more disappointment. Holy Spirit, bring up the hidden pain, the bitter root judgments I've made about life. As they surface, I give them to you. I choose to hope again, to dream again, to listen to your direction. I ask you to put my feet on the path of life again. Purify my desires. May I fulfill all that you wrote in your book for me. Amen

Deliverance To Freedom

THE VOICE IN THE SHOWER

A friend and I decided to attend a conference in Washington, D.C. We had attended one meeting, spent the night in a hotel and were getting ready the next morning to return to the conference. I was in the shower when I heard the Lord speak to me, "You aren't here to go to that conference. You are here to get your mom's destiny back." I knew mom had worked in D.C. during World War II for a Navy general. Her job was to send weapons to combat zones. Prior to getting the job, she had taken a Civil Service exam and scored high enough to be offered the job in D.C. I'm not sure how long she worked there, but I know it wasn't long. Her mother, my grandmother, asked her to return home to Missouri to help her on the farm. Mom was the oldest of nine children, and the only one who was not living at home at the time. In obedience to her mother, my mom quit her job in D.C. and returned to the farm.

I told my friend, Judy, what the Lord had said to me and we decided to skip the conference to do some research. We went to the Library of Congress to search for information. We found out that the temporary war-related office buildings were erected on the Washington Mall in 1941, but were later torn down by the Eisenhower Administration. We looked through pictures of the era, trying to find clues to solving the mystery of the job my mom had left.

After hours of research, I asked the Lord to help us find keys to retrieve the destiny my mom left behind. I asked for more confirmation of this assignment. We decided to call the Navy information line to see if they had any more information about the location of the office buildings or the general she had worked for. We found the Navy phone number and discovered that the last four digits of the information line were the last four digits of my mother's phone number. I heard the Lord say, "Do you need more confirmation or will that suffice?" Nope - that was enough for us!

We decided to walk to the place where the temporary WWII buildings had been. There I found a willow tree, sat down under it, and wept over the loss of family destiny. You see, I believe we have a personal book written for each of us, but also a family line purpose to fulfill.

I asked the Lord to restore what had been lost. It was an experience I will never forget. While in prayer under that willow tree, I saw the scroll of her destiny hanging in mid-air. I reached up, retrieved it, and accepted its assignments into my life. Since that time, I have been given many prayer assignments in D.C. Doors have opened for sending prayer teams to fourteen different nations of the world.

The Lord is faithful to restore what we have lost, including time. It's never too late to retrieve lost dreams. Don't forget the story of the twelve spies sent into the promised land. Ten came back with an evil report. Joshua and Caleb believed God that the land could be taken. Because ten spies did not believe, a generation died in the wilderness, but God was faithful to Joshua and Caleb. The ten spies who did not believe God for victory against their enemies died without fulfillment of what had been promised.

> *But my servant Caleb has a different attitude than the others have. He has remained loyal to me, so I will bring him into the land he explored. His descendants will possess their full share of that land.*

> Numbers 14:24 NLT

Don't allow your dreams to be stolen by the naysayers, the doubters, the deceived. It's OK to dream big dreams with God. Don't allow disappointments to lodge in your heart. You are a child of God with a purpose to fulfill. Defeat the enemies of doubt, fear, and disappointment. Write your dreams down. Remind God of His promises to you. Rise above the settler mentality and pioneer new territory for God. He put those dreams in your heart. As long as they line up with the plumb line of His word, pursue with determination those dreams. Cry out as Caleb did, "Give me this mountain!"

> *"As yet I am as strong this day as on the day that Moses sent me; just as my strength was then, so now is my strength for war, both for going out and for coming in. Now therefore, give me this mountain of which the LORD spoke in that day; for you heard in that day how the Anakim were there, and that the cities were great and fortified. It may be that the LORD will be with me, and I shall be able to drive them out as the LORD said." And Joshua blessed him, and gave Hebron to Caleb the son of Jephunneh as an inheritance. Hebron therefore became the inheritance of Caleb the son of Jephunneh the Kenizzite to this day, because he wholly followed the LORD God of Israel.*

Joshua 14:11-14 NKJV

Caleb fell victim to the choice of the unbelieving ten spies, but their choice only delayed Caleb's fulfillment—it did not destroy it. God demonstrated His faithfulness to Caleb allowing him to retain the strength of his youth. Retrieve your dreams. Know that God is faithful. Circumstances may have delayed your promises and dreams, but God is faithful.

Lord, I want to retrieve what has been lost, both to me and my family. I don't want to walk through life never finding my purpose. Don't allow me to wander in the wilderness of doubt, disappointment, and hope deferred. Give me a Caleb heart to believe you over the circumstances around me. Give me my mountain, my inheritance. Don't let me settle for less than you have purposed for me. I choose to live in obedience to your Spirit. I know your purposes for me will bring the abundant life you promised. Dream your dreams through me. I trust your leading more than the disappointments I have experienced. Amen.

Deliverance To Freedom

5

The Crimson Door

*In fact, the law requires that nearly everything be
cleansed with blood, and without the shedding of
blood there is no forgiveness.*

Hebrews 9:22 NIV

*I am the door; if anyone enters through Me, he
will be saved, and will go in and out and find
pasture.*

John 10:9 NASB

In John 10:9 (above), Jesus describes Himself as the door. A door
is an entrance and an exit. Jesus is the entrance into life and
the exit from bondage. Most of us have seen the movie, The Ten
Commandments (1959) based on the Old Testament account of
the deliverance of Israel from Egypt. In one scene, the Israelites
take branches of hyssop and paint lamb's blood on the doorposts
and lintel of the entrance to their homes. The death angel was
about to kill the firstborn of each household, but would pass over
any house where the blood had been applied.

Moreover, they shall take some of the blood and put it on the two doorposts and on the lintel of the houses in which they eat it.

Exodus 12:7 NASB

The doorposts are the two vertical pieces of timber on either side of the entrance. Merriam-webster defines lintel as: "a horizontal architectural member spanning and usually carrying the load above an opening." (https://www.merriam-webster.com/dictionary/lentil)

According to Merriam-Webster, there are load-bearing lintels and ornamental, decorative lintels.

I believe the door painted with blood represented the coming crucifixion. The wooden doorposts became the wooden cross, and the lintel, the structure that held the entrance in place, was Jesus Himself. He is not an ornamental lintel, a man on a cross to decorate a wall in a house or church. *"He is before all things, and in Him all things hold together"* (Colossians 1:17). He is the doorpost, the lintel, and the entrance. His blood is the Lamb's blood that holds death at bay. When we enter through the Door, we enter into life. With His blood painted on the doorposts of our heart, we are safe in Him. Passover was a prophetic picture of the door to life, who is Jesus. The door was painted with the blood of the Passover lamb.

The power of that blood to protect, heal, and deliver applies to us individually, and to cities, states, and nations. I can see the doorposts of our family, our bloodline, painted with the blood of the Lamb of God. Hopefully, your family has the blood painted on your doorposts as well. The principles of freedom for individuals, families, and lands are the same. Outside of the protection of God, we are prey for the enemy. The covenant we have with God, sealed with His own blood, frees us personally and corporately from destruction.

THE GAZEBO

We took a team to a city in our state of Missouri that was dealing with demonic oppression and attacks on its spiritual leadership. The pastors of the city had been struck with sickness, divorce, and disunity. We had previously prayer walked the college in the city. We left there to scout out the rest of the city, stopping at several places, and ending up at the city park. The fountain that had once been a focal point of the park was dry. The park was in disrepair. We decided to return to the park in a couple of weeks with a worship team to hold a prayer and worship gathering purposing to change the oppressive atmosphere. We secured permission from the city to hold an outdoor gathering there.

As I spoke to the Lord about the city, He reminded me of the lamb's blood painted on the doorposts that caused the death angel to pass over. He instructed our team to take Missouri wine, representing His blood, and place it on the doorposts of the gazebo in the park, declaring His blood defeats the death structures of sickness and oppression in the city. He also instructed us to pour water in the dry fountain decreeing the water of life will flow through this city once again. We also took wooden stakes with scriptures on them to place in the ground, to plant seeds of His Word for harvest.

The day came for the worship event in the center of the city park. The worship began. We sang and freely worshipped, openly giving glory to our King. The time came to apply the wine to the doorposts of the gazebo, representing the doorposts of the city. Suddenly a demonic man came walking through the park, confronted us and tried to disrupt our gathering. He walked up the steps of the gazebo, trying to give me tarot cards, and yelling at us. We continued to worship and commanded the demonic spirits to leave. He dropped his tarot cards and left the park. We then applied the wine to the posts and decreed life to the city. We found a trash container and burned the tarot cards decreeing spiritual knowledge from the dark side would no longer have access. It was time to place our stakes in the ground. We found an old oak tree, took our stakes with the scriptures written on them, and our hammer. We tried and tried to pound the stakes in the hard ground. We couldn't do it. Suddenly, we heard the sound of motorcycles enter the park. A group of Christian motorcyclists pulled up, drove up to our tree which was growing by the road that led into the park, and asked what we were doing. We told them what we were doing with the stakes, but we couldn't get them in the hard ground. One of the men said, "Give me that hammer." They took turns pounding our stakes into the hard soil. When they finished the job, they got on their motorcycles, drove off and disappeared. I've often wondered if angels ride motorcycles, show up at the right time, pound stakes in the ground and drive off into the sunset.

> *Lord, I thank you that the blood of Jesus is a weapon against death structures in our families, cities, states, and the nations of the world. The blood protects, gives life, defeats our enemies, and transfers us out of darkness into life. The blood cleanses us from sin and shame, causes our enemies to flee, and brings us into life eternal.*

The Crimson Door

You are the door. You are our Passover lamb. I apply the blood to the doorposts of our family. Thank you that your blood defeats sickness and disease. I renew my covenant with you, taking into my body the bread, representing your broken body, taking into my body, the wine, representing your blood. Thank you for freeing us from every work of darkness. Amen

THE MASSACRE SITE

Periodically, the Lord gives specific assignments in other nations. I've been to Bosnia and Herzegovina, land of the Balkans, three times, taking trained teams to pray on site to free the land from oppression. It is a beautiful nation of mountains and rivers, a bridge nation between eastern and western Europe. A little background will help in understanding the weight of the prayer assignment I am about to describe.

World War I started on a bridge in 1914 in Sarajevo, the nation's Capital, when a Bosnian Serb student, Gavrilo Princip, assassinated the Austrian archduke Franz Ferdinand. This precipitated World War I. I've stood on that bridge interceding for wars to cease and the destiny of that nation to come forth. Conflict has plagued this territory for many years.

The Bosnia civil war, 1991-1995, a complex conflict that resulted in "an estimated 100,000 people who were killed, 80% of whose were Bosnians. In 1995, Bosnian Serb forces killed as many as 8,000 Bosnian men and boys from the town of Srebrenica. It was the largest massacre in

Deliverance To Freedom

Europe since the Holocaust.

https://www.ushmm.org/confront-genocide/cases/
bosnia-herzegovina

The Siege of Sarajevo was the longest siege of a capital city in the history of modern warfare. After being initially besieged by the forces of the Yugoslav People's Army, Sarajevo, the capital of Bosnia and Herzegovina, was besieged by the Army of Republika Srpska from 5 April 1992 to 29 February 1996 (1,425 days) during the Bosnian War. The siege lasted three times longer than the Battle of Stalingrad and more than a year longer than the Siege of Leningrad.

https://en.m.wikipedia.org/wiki/Siege of Sarajevo

In 2004, our team arrived in Sarajevo, the main international airport, landing on the short runway in the valley between the mountains. Flying in, you could see the mountainside with quaint homes, smoke rising from chimneys, and as we approached the city, closely stacked white stucco houses with red roofs. Later, as we drove through the city, we observed many buildings with riveted bullet holes remaining from the siege of the city during the war. As you leave the city, half-finished houses dotted the landscape. Building a home for your children was the goal. For many of the people, it was financially impossible to build a home for themselves, so they worked for years to provide shelter, hoping to finish it for their children to occupy.

When I take a team into a nation for a prayer assignment, the team has been trained to work together with a corporate anointing.

They are prepared physically and spiritually, have secured Intercessors to pray for the assignment, and recognize they are not on a vacation. The team is apostolically sent, commissioned, and prayed over prior to leaving the states. We always connect with spiritual gatekeepers in the targeted nation, acquiring their permission and agreement with our decrees over their nation. Our assignments are not just good ideas, but Holy Spirit directed.

One of our specific assignments in Bosnia was to pray over a massacre site of mass graves. Part of the perseverance needed was just finding the place. We did not have a guide, nor an interpreter. We rented a van; one of our team members was the driver. We bought a map, and off we went. A young worship leader positioned herself in the back of the van leading us in worship as we searched out our target. After several hours of driving and searching, we found the site. We gathered together in front of a small chapel, perceiving the spiritual atmosphere of the place. I wanted to feel what God was feeling, to see what He saw and to stand between heaven and earth, for His purposes in that nation.

Suddenly, I heard the blood of those who had been unjustly murdered, cry out from the ground. This is a Biblical concept. When Cain killed his brother, Abel, the Lord told Cain that his brother's blood was crying out from the ground.

> *The LORD said, "What have you done? Listen! Your brother's blood cries out to me from the ground.*
>
> Genesis 4:10 NIV

The roar of the cry of blood from the mass grave was deafening. I then saw a vision of drops of blood, each with a mouth wide open crying out for justice. All of us on the team were bent over in intercession for the remedy to this injustice. "Lord, what is the answer to this cry? We are here! We are standing for your purposes for this nation. What do we do?" I clearly heard Him speak the answer: "Put the covenant of life represented by the blood of my Son in the mouths that are crying out for justice." We took the elements of the covenant, the bread and the wine, partook of it ourselves positioning the team under the protection of the covenant of life that breaks covenants with death. We then dropped pieces of bread, and poured wine into the land seeing it placed in the mouths of those who had been unjustly slain.

> *...and they cried out with a loud voice, saying, "How long, O Lord, holy and true, will You refrain from judging and avenging our blood on those who dwell on the earth?"*

> Revelation 6:10 NIV

We heard the voice of God's Spirit instructing us. "The only answer to the voice of the blood crying out from the ground is the blood of my Son." The deafening cry for justice was silenced by the answer.

I've had a hesitancy to write about what happened in this place. It was life changing and very meaningful to all of us who were there. We don't take lightly the assignments given to us by the Lord, nor do we claim some kind of fame or super Christian persona over ourselves. The reality of what happened cannot be denied by those of us who were there. The spirit realm is real, and the power of God cannot be denied once you have experienced it.

We finished our assignment there by decreeing Isaiah 62 over the nation of Bosnia.

For Zion's sake I will not keep silent, and for Jerusalem's sake I will not keep quiet, Until her righteousness goes forth like brightness, and her salvation like a torch that is burning. The nations will see your righteousness, and all kings your glory; and you will be called by a new name Which the mouth of the LORD will designate. You will also be a crown of beauty in the hand of the LORD, and a royal diadem in the hand of your God. It will no longer be said to you, "Forsaken," Nor to your land will it any longer be said, "Desolate"; But you will be called, "My delight is in her," and your land, "Married"; For the LORD delights in you, and to Him your land will be married. For as a young man marries a virgin, so your sons will marry you; and as the bridegroom rejoices over the bride, so your God will rejoice over you. On your walls, O Jerusalem, I have appointed watchmen; all day and all night they will never keep silent. You who remind the LORD, take no rest for yourselves; and give Him no rest until He establishes and makes Jerusalem a praise in the earth. The LORD has sworn by His right hand and by His strong arm, "I will never again give your grain as food for your enemies; nor will foreigners drink your new wine for which you have labored." But those who garner it will eat it and praise the LORD; and those who gather it will drink it in the courts of My sanctuary. Go through, go through the gates, clear the way for the people; build up, build up the highway, remove the stones, lift up a standard over the peoples. Behold, the LORD has proclaimed to the end of the earth, say to the daughter of Zion, "Lo, your salvation comes; behold His reward is with Him, and His recompense before Him." And they will call them, "The holy people, the redeemed of the LORD "; and you will be called, "Sought out, a city not forsaken."

Isaiah 62

The power of the blood covenant cannot be underestimated. The covenant of life in Christ Jesus is greater than covenants with death. When we are outside the protection of His covenant, we can be vulnerable to our adversary, who is seeking someone to devour. When we stand in intercession for people or territories, the power of the voice of the blood of Jesus puts our enemy on the run. There is no deliverance without recognition and acceptance of the blood sacrifice of Jesus Christ, the Lamb of God, who takes away the sin of the world.

6

Who Are You?

Jesus knew that the Father had put all things under his power, and that he had come from God and was returning to God; so he got up from the meal, took off his outer clothing, and wrapped a towel around his waist. After that, he poured water into a basin and began to wash his disciples' feet, drying them with the towel that was wrapped around him.

John 13:3-5 NIV

I remember the day we received a letter from the IRS. Someone we did not know had filed our taxes. The IRS sent a letter to confirm some of the details. We took the letter to our accountant who put an end to the confusion by calling the IRS. No one wants a letter from the Internal Revenue Service, let alone one that confirms someone else has filed your return.

A friend of mine, who is well known in ministry circles, had his Facebook account duplicated by an unknown thief, who promptly set up a donate button to obtain money. The hacker was discovered and stopped before he benefited from the scenario.

In our city, there is a person who has the same name as mine. My husband went to the bank to deposit money in my account. After several days, it did not show up. We called the bank and asked about it, giving them my account number. They couldn't find it either, but eventually traced it. It had been deposited into another Regina Shank's account. Will the real Regina Shank please stand up? I did stand up and claim what was mine.

I took a team to Israel. We arrived at the Tel Aviv airport where we went through security. One of our team members was detained for several hours because he had the same name as a smuggler they were looking for.

Sometimes we must prove our identity to the world, and there are times we must protect that same identity from thieves who want to steal what is rightfully ours. Your name is a label by which you are identified. Your voice identifies you. Your fingerprints are uniquely your own. But who are you in the core of your identity? Your identity is important.

Identity is both internal and external in its substance. I believe the internal identity we possess influences the external persona displayed to the natural world. Dictionary.com defines identity as:

> *"a condition or character as to who a person or what a thing is; the qualities, beliefs, etc., that distinguish or identify a person or thing:"*

http://www.dictionary.com/browse/identity

Mistaken identity plagues humanity. External labels can tattoo us internally; external circumstances can become the forms that shape our lives into grotesque miniatures of who we were meant to be. But at our core, we were designed to represent the Father—as sons and daughters birthed into a new identity, adopted, selected, apprehended from a fallen world system, transformed into new creations, changed internally to demonstrate externally who we are. Your identity is not in what you do or in what has happened to you. Your identity is not found in the labels given you by family, friends, or enemies.

I remember the day I was removing labels from the bottom of 100 Libby glasses I had purchased for my son's wedding rehearsal dinner. (Don't ask me why I didn't use an easier method.) I was standing by the sink filled with warm sudsy water with 100 glasses lined up for washing. I had a bottle of Goo-Be-Gone standing by just in case it was needed. I washed each glass scraping off the label. About half way through the process, I heard the Lord speak to me, "I've called you to remove labels from my people."

I realized at that moment that the Lord had removed many labels from my life. The label on the bottom of the Libby glass identified the manufacturer. The labels on my life identified my journey like stickers on a traveling trunk. I had been to the land of rejection and labeled such by the experiences. My traveling trunk carried the label of: "a mouth to feed not a voice to listen to." Consequently, I talked little fearing it would come out wrong, and I would be devalued even more. I'm not trying to glorify where I've been, rather I am testifying to the ability of God to remove false identity labels and transform us into the identity He planned for us before the foundation of the world. I continued removing labels until all 100 Libby glasses were ready for the wedding. These were clean vessels, ready to contain refreshing beverages for our guests.

The Sunday after the wedding, I was scheduled to speak at

the morning service of a nearby church. As I was speaking, I kept noticing a young lady sitting in the back row. I knew the Lord had a word of encouragement for her, so at the end of the message, I asked the young lady to stand up. I said, "I believe the Lord has a word for you. You came today because you are searching. What is your name?"

In a quiet voice, she said, "My name is Libby."

After removing 100 labels from Libby glasses, and hearing the Lord tell me I was called to remove labels from His people, I knew this Libby had been labeled by her circumstances, her friends, and by her own attitude toward herself. I spoke to her, "The Lord says, you have been labeled by others, by your experiences, by your own beliefs about yourself. He is removing from your life the labels of rejection, failure, abandonment, valueless, and ugly. You have traveled through that foreign territory, but now you are home, safe in His protection. He loves you and has called you into a new identity as His daughter. You came expecting to be overlooked, expecting to bear the pain of your past for the rest of your life, but God says He is embracing you right now, and removing the indentations in your soul put there by the harsh words and the circumstances you have endured. You are His Libby, and He will fill your vessel with clean, pure water. Many will taste of the water of Life through you. This is your day of transformation!"

Libby allowed the body of Christ to embrace her. She received the love she had longed to experience and Jesus found her that day. Allow Him to find you today. You are not a throw-away person. You are not the ugly step-child, the unwanted one, the sick one, the old one, the one with no talent. You are not the poor one, the failure, the felon, the divorcee, the stupid one, the fat one.

Who Are You?

It's time to throw off the false identity labels that have kept us in bondage for years. We can even carry an identity of a particular sickness or disease. I've heard people embrace their sickness like it's who they are instead of what they are overcoming. They call it "my diabetes," "my handicap," "my cancer." None of those diseases are ours to possess. I should not accept what the Lord said He has overcome. And we should no longer use negative labels to our advantage, trying to get attention, and sympathy from them.

A middle-aged woman walked into our food ministry and declared to me she was handicapped, so she needed to be first in line to get the food basket we were giving away. I said to her, "You don't look handicapped."

"Well, I am!" She said.

"We have some comfortable seats over there." I pointed to our tables and chairs. "Here is your number. We will call you up here in a few minutes."

"You don't believe I'm handicapped, do you? I have my certificate out in the car. I'm going to go get it, so you will believe me." She walled sprightly out the door to get her certificate of handicap-ism to prove that her disability, and the reason she could not stand in line, was real.

There is a fighter in me that refuses to accept false labels, false identity, or a handicapped mentality. Using our adversities as a ticket to the front of the line is contrary to the ways of God. He said in Luke:

"When someone invites you to a wedding feast, do not take the place of honor, for a person more distinguished than you may have been

invited. If so, the host who invited both of you will come and say to you, 'Give this person your seat.' Then, humiliated, you will have to take the least important place. But when you are invited, take the lowest place, so that when your host comes, he will say to you, 'Friend, move up to a better place.' Then you will be honored in the presence of all the other guests. For all those who exalt themselves will be humbled, and those who humble themselves will be exalted."

Luke 14:8-12 NIV

Jesus knew who He was, but was interested to know who people thought he was.

And it happened that while He was praying alone, the disciples were with Him, and He questioned them, saying, "Who do the people say that I am?" They answered and said, "John the Baptist, and others say Elijah; but others, that one of the prophets of old has risen again." And He said to them, "But who do you say that I am?" And Peter answered and said, "The Christ of God."

Luke 9:18-20 NASB

Internally, the Son of God was secure in His identity. He knew where He came from and knew where He was going. That's why He could take a towel and wash the feet of others. But He wanted others to grasp His identity.

Jesus, knowing who He was, humbled Himself, took the towel

and washed His disciple's feet. People who demand a place do not know who they are, nor where they are going.

We were not made to be reactors to our circumstances or to the people around us. We are called to respond to each situation by the Spirit of God. Rejection is your enemy; the person who rejected you is not. Abandonment is your enemy; the people who abandoned you are not. Addiction and hopelessness are your enemies. We do not fight flesh and blood, but principalities and powers. Instead of looking inward, look up. The Lord is willing and able to change you from the inside out. Trust Him! Your wayward life is not His fault. Remember, it's a fallen world. We can fall victim of other people's choices, but we don't have to stay that way. You can overcome what has been sent to destroy you with the grace and power found in your relationship with God, through His Son Jesus Christ. Sit before the Lord; present yourself to Him as one in need of His healing grace.

PRAYER

Here I am Lord. I need you. I have blamed everyone and everything for my present condition. Here I sit overcome by feelings of rejection, abandonment, unworthiness, shame. You have overcoming power for me. I reach out to you with all my heart, holding nothing back. You know what I've been through. It's not your fault. Wash me, cleanse me of my past. Bathe me in your love. Touch every wound; remove the scabbed over façade I display to the world. Open up my wounds, pour in your loving disinfectant.

Let healing begun, proceed, and be completed. You are the Great Physician! Heal the eyes of my heart, so I can see the real enemies of my soul. I decree with Joseph what he said to his brothers who betrayed him in Genesis:

"As for you, you meant evil against me, but God meant it for good in order to bring about this present result, to preserve many people alive."

Genesis 50:20 NASB

Lord, you will cause me to overcome. The power of my will is greater than the power of my feelings. I submit my will and my feelings to the work of your Spirit. I forgive my abusers. They were victims themselves. I know who I am now, your child created to demonstrate your glory in the earth. I am the clay; you are the potter. Make me a vessel that pours out clean, pure water from the Life you have restored within me. I set myself in agreement with your word from Isaiah:

Behold, God is my salvation, I will trust and not be afraid; For the LORD GOD is my strength and song, and He has become my salvation. Therefore you will joyously draw water from the springs of salvation. And in that day you will say, "Give thanks to the LORD, call on His name. Make known His deeds among the peoples; Make them remember that His name is exalted." Praise the

Deliverance To Freedom

58

Who Are You?

LORD in song, for He has done excellent things;
Let this be known throughout the earth. Cry
aloud and shout for joy, O inhabitant of Zion, for
great in your midst is the Holy One of Israel.

Isaiah 12:2-6 NASB

IDENTITY DECLARATIONS

- I am a tree firmly planted by streams of water which yields fruit in its season, my leaves will not wither, and whatever I do, will prosper. (ref. Psalm 1:3)

- I am a vessel of honor, created for my Master's use.

- I am no longer a slave to fear, addiction, rejection, jealousy, or deception. The Lord has adopted me as His child. I am bathed in His love, and His Truth shields me from false expectations of myself and others.

- I am not trapped in adverse circumstances. Jesus is the door, the way out. He is also the way into rest, restoration, and healing. I am His workmanship. He will complete the work He has begun in me.

- I am not who I think I am; I am not who people say I am; I am who God says I am.

- I am valued, purchased by Jesus' blood, and transformed into a new identity as His child.

- I have a Father who loves me. I am no longer fatherless, uncared for or unwanted. The Lord has chosen me as His own. My boundary lines have been set by His love.

- I will no longer wander in dark places with no place to rest. Lord, I cast my cares on You, because You care for me.

Deliverance To Freedom

- My times are in the hands of God. I will not get ahead of Him, nor will I walk behind. I will keep in step with His plan for me, conquering each obstacle in my path by His power.

- I know who I am now. I choose to know Jesus and make His name known in the earth.

- I am a worshipper of Jesus, not a spectator. I am activated by His spirit within me to walk the path of life laid out for me.

- The dark paths of my past are not who I am. My identity is not in my experiences but is found in His love for me.

- I am a new creation in Christ. Old things have passed away. All things have become new.

7

Who Are You - External Props

Jesus saw Nathanael coming toward Him, and said of him, "Here is an Israelite indeed [a true descendant of Jacob], in whom there is no guile nor deceit nor duplicity!"

John 1:47

The definition of duplicity, a synonym of guile, is: "deceitfulness in speech or conduct, as by speaking or acting in two different ways to different people concerning the same matter; double-dealing."

http://www.dictionary.com/browse/duplicity

Jesus could see right through Nathanael. A transparent person like Nathanael doesn't hide behind a title or position, nor claim importance through the important people he might hang out with. He was genuine in speech, attitude, and marked by integrity. He meant what he said, and said what he meant.

I remember the day a friend of mine walked into my office to show off his new haircut. The barber had shaved all the hair off of his head. He took off his hat and said, "How do you like it?" I didn't like it at all. He had a very nice head of hair, which I thought was complimentary to his appearance. Internally, I was considering statements like, "Wow, that's nice!" Or "I'm sure your hat fits better." Or "Hopefully, it will grow back quickly."

I wanted to compliment him, but knew I had to make an authentic statement in order to be true to myself. I said something like, "It certainly changed your appearance."

He turned to leave, smiled and said, "Yeah, isn't it great?"

Being truthful is important to me. I've never enjoyed being lied to, nor have I allowed myself to lie to others. I have, however, lied to myself. I've listed a few of those lies that kept me running a race with no finishing line. Hopefully, none of the lies following have impacted your life like they did mine.

- If you work hard enough, you will be valued for what you produce.

- When you have friends over to your home, it has to be in perfect order, or you will be rejected.

- You need to be recognized for your accomplishments. That will give you value.

- You have to look good, smell good, act appropriately, say the right thing, meet every deadline, and bake a cake for the bake sale or you are not valuable.

- You have to earn your place in the world, so run Regina, run, accomplish, produce, make it happen.

- The end result of this deceitful, internal belief system was exhaustion.

Eventually, I learned that value is received, not produced by meaningful or meaningless activities. I eventually removed myself from the treadmill of performance, after my superwoman persona met the kryptonite of impossible odds. I was married, raising three children, working part time at a bank, writing and directing the junior miss pageant, served as president of the PTA, room mother for my daughter's elementary school class, helped at the school carnival, and produced a delicious homemade meal each evening for my family. Oh, and don't forget helping the children with homework, taking them to school and picking them up afterward, and having a semblance of a prayer life. I appeared to the outside world to be in charge of my life, but I was dying on the inside. It all fell apart the day I found myself in the bathroom, sliding down the wall to the floor, in a heap of emotion crying out to God for help. Needless to say, the Lord delivered me from a false self and gave me a new identity in Him. I received His unconditional love for me. He eradicated the lies that almost destroyed me, and gave me peace in my relationship with a Father who accepted me, loved me, and valued me, even if I never did another thing to prove my worth.

The question to consider as you read this chapter is: "Have you discovered the Father's plan for your life?" That discovery will change your life as you realize you are not here to wander through deserts of pain, finally discovering an occasional, temporary oasis. You are here to walk out a Divine orchestrated, plan for your life. I didn't discover His plan for me until all my plans shattered to the earth like pieces of glass; until self-effort rendered no return on its promises.

Identity is a core issue when it comes to freedom. Living life from a false self requires constant energy to keep up the charade. It also motivates accusation against others who do not treat us with the respect we think we have earned. Respect is an internal attitude flowing from a healed identity. Respect for oneself negates the need to demand it from others. Respect begets respect. Honor begets honor. A wounded identity demands recognition from others. Knowing who you are, allows you to sit on a back row without complaint, to serve others without feeling it's demeaning, to rejoice when someone else is blessed, to remain silent when others claim ownership of that which originated from you.

The seventy, eighty, ninety years we have on this planet have been planned and purposed from the heart of a loving Father, who determined the place and time you would arrive, determined the length of your days, and wrote destiny in a book with your name on it.

> "And He made from one man every nation of mankind to live on all the face of the earth, having determined their appointed times and the boundaries of their habitation, that they would seek God, if perhaps they might grope for Him and find Him, though He is not far from each one of us; for in Him we live and move and exist, as even some of your own poets have said, 'For we also are His children.'"
>
> Acts 17:26-28 NASB

> "My frame was not hidden from You, When I was made in secret,
>
> And skillfully wrought in the depths of the earth; Your eyes have seen my unformed substance;
>
> And in Your book were all written The days that

were ordained for me,

When as yet there was not one of them."

Psalms 139:15-16

The world is full of external pursuits, some of which can be successfully conquered to advance our future. But when those degrees, titles, ordination papers, famous ancestors, or famous friends become credentials to prove our worth, we have an identity problem. Your value as a person was established when the Son of God demonstrated your merit by purchasing you with His own blood.

People in the body of Christ who try to find an identity by claiming a title like prophet, apostle, or pastor and then try to live up to that claim, may think an external title will give them credibility or cure their rejection issues. Even a genuine title is not an identity, but a gift given to steward. Titles are not claimed, but are given because a gift is recognized and given credibility with a title. Gifts are given by God and five fold ministry leaders are appointed by God. The genuine gift is recognized by others, identified and released through commissioning. To know God and make Him known is a noble pursuit. If a title comes with it, great. If not, it is enough to be known by the King.

WHO ARE YOU?

Are you formed and fashioned by the culture around you? Are you like the chameleon, changing your appearance to fit the situation? Are you trying to earn your place in this world? Are you longing to be heard or choosing not to say a word for fear of rejection? The image designed for your life has already been created. Discovering your book, written by the Father for you, can be a lifelong pursuit, or you can allow it to pursue you. When I quit running, grasping, striving, longing, desperately trying to reach the unreachable, I found a loving father waiting for me with book in hand, and power afoot, to carry me into desire fulfilled and purpose realized.

Identity is not earned; it is received. The truth is, you are royalty! Your Father is King of the universe. You were created in His image to represent Him in the earth. You are called to know Him and make Him known. You have been adopted into His family. There is a place at His table with your name on it. The world offers what it cannot give. You are different! Eternity resides in your heart. You can conform to external modifiers of your identity or you can receive internal transformation through revelation from His Spirit. Rejection and fear can be the slave masters of your soul, or you can break out of their grasp. Knowing the truth will set you free. Pray this prayer with me. The cell door is open. Freedom awaits!

> *Father, I choose to come out of a false identity. I remove myself from the treadmill of performance. I have run from shame, rejection, and fear. I want to come home to the safety of my Father's house. I have been the prodigal, taking my inheritance and spending it on foolish pleasures, pleasures that have left me empty, depleted, and dry. My dehydrated soul thirsts for the water of life you provide. My rejected heart longs to be embraced by your love. Your word says, in your Presence is fullness of joy and at your right hand there are pleasures evermore. I choose to seek first your*

Kingdom and your righteousness and all these other things I have been pursuing will be added to me. Forgive me for seeking the things I thought I needed instead of seeking you. You have the rest, refreshment, and strength I need. Give me understanding of who I really am. The image of Jesus Christ dwells in my heart. I lay down the false images the world has offered me. Here I am Lord. I ask you for my book of destiny. You wrote my life story before I was born. I tried to write my own story; it has culminated in tragedy. I trade its torn pages and distorted illustrations for the classic literary creation that has my name on it. Show me who I am. I choose your plan and purpose for my life. Empower me with your acceptance and love. I come home to you Father, God. Amen.

Deliverance To Freedom

8

The Bitter Root

*You will go out in joy and be led forth in peace;
the mountains and hills will burst into song
before you, and all the trees of the field will clap
their hands. Instead of the thorn bush will grow
the juniper, and instead of briers the myrtle will
grow. This will be for the LORD's renown, for an
everlasting sign, that will endure forever."*

Isaiah 55:12-13 NIV

It grew from a seed. The predator took root and its thorny branches grew into tangled briers of long forgotten offenses. Its roots invaded the soil of the relationship, leaving little room for the garden of intimacy to survive. Bitterness enters the day the offense takes place.

Several years ago, I started a women's ministry to regional women. We had our own worship team, held a monthly outreach gathering, hosted retreats and dinners, inviting inspirational speakers to bring encouragement to the ladies. We were experiencing growth. Women were driving in from surrounding cities to experience the power of Holy Spirit in their lives. We held the meetings in our church, but it was not under the jurisdiction of the church. Things were going well until part of my leadership team went to my pastor and complained about me. They said I held the reins too tightly and they wanted him to straighten me out. I had no idea they were upset, and no clue they were complaining to my pastor at the same time I was speaking and praying for women. He graciously supported me and told them to come directly to me.

The three of them asked me to meet them at the church. They surrounded me on all sides and began to tell me everything that was wrong with my leadership. It was a total surprise to me. I remember feeling like I had been punched in the stomach. It was three against one. When one finished with me, another would start, then another would step in to enlarge on the subject. When they finished the critique, they asked me for a response. I had none. I remember thinking that if I defend myself, I would be taking the Lord's place as my defender. If I gave them what they wanted, I would be releasing to them what the Lord had birthed through me. I told them I would talk to the Lord about their concerns. They left, and I dropped to my knees in disbelief. These were my friends! At this point, I was having trouble breathing. It felt like my airway was cut off.

I went home and stared into space in disbelief. After a while, I called a friend to ask for prayer. I knew even though I didn't want to open my heart to anyone, I had to, in order to get past the devastation of it all. In talking to her, we decided I needed to get away for a couple of days. Three other leadership women and I drove to a lake condo that one of them owned. For two days, we sought the Lord, worshipped, spent time in prayer together and also personal time with Jesus. They ended up praying for me. I still felt like the air was being squeezed out of me like a boa constrictor was around my waist.

They seated me in a chair and prayed for me, commanding the restrictive force to let me go. After much prayer, I felt it leave, and I could breathe again. Believe me, it was difficult to submit myself to their prayers a few days after the traumatic episode with the other three friends. I wanted to isolate from everyone. I wanted to give up ministry. After a couple of days away, I was somewhat better and we returned to our homes.

The next day I was spending time with the Lord. I was sitting in a chair in my living room. The Lord spoke to me out of Song of Solomon:

> I opened for my beloved, but my beloved had left;
> he was gone. My heart sank at his departure. I
> looked for him but did not find him. I called him
> but he did not answer. The watchmen found me
> as they made their rounds in the city. They beat
> me, they bruised me; they took away my cloak,
> those watchmen of the walls!
>
> Song of Songs 5:6-7 NIV

As I read that scripture, I realized I couldn't stop my pursuit of the Lover of my soul. I knew He was worth any persecution or criticism I might experience. I read on.

> Where has your beloved gone, most beautiful of
> women? Which way did your beloved turn, that
> we may look for him with you? My beloved has
> gone down to his garden, to the beds of spices, to
> browse in the gardens and to gather lilies.
>
> Song of Songs 6:1-2 NIV

Deliverance To Freedom

My heart was stirred. I repented of my vow to never do women's ministry again. I found solace in His presence. Suddenly, I found myself in a garden. It was beautiful; flowers were everywhere. A sparkling brook that seemed to sing as it bubbled its way though the polished stones caught my attention. I was looking at it when I became aware that Jesus was standing next to me. We sat down on a stone bench that suddenly appeared. I don't remember what He said to me, but I do remember the love I felt, and the peace I experienced in that garden. I know physically I did not leave my chair, but I also know I was in that garden. I can't explain it. I don't have to.

A few days later, I was communicating with the Lord and He asked me a question. "What do you want me to do to those three women who hurt you?"

Wow! What a question? I know now He was revealing what was in my heart. I replied. "Give me a minute, Lord."

I sat there for a while, thinking about what I could say. At that moment, I had to discern if I had really forgiven them, if I had let go of offense, if I still had anger toward them. After a few moments, I responded, "Lord, I want You to bless them. Bless them with Your Presence. Bless them with the desires of their heart. Bless their finances, their future, their families. I sincerely want You to bless them."

I was free! Their words of criticism had encased my emotions, shut off my life flow, and constricted my forward movement. I didn't feel like forgiving. I didn't feel like they deserved a blessing. But my choice to let it go, to forgive and bless, brought me into the freedom I needed. I was free from the cell of bitterness and the chains of unforgiveness. I had wanted to run from people to isolate from the body of Christ. I hadn't wanted to trust myself to close friendships. All of that left when I chose to forgive and bless.

One of the women who hurt me moved away. I tried to reconcile, but she would not answer my calls or respond to the card I sent. That was difficult for me. I wanted to make it right again. I finally had to let it go. Another one had an affair with her neighbor's husband, left the church and lost her family. The third one distanced herself and is still trying to find her place.

As for the ministry, it continued to grow and impacted women all over the region. They learned to pray, work together bearing each other's burdens. Many of them raised up prayer and Bible Study groups in their own cities. Some went on to establish their own ministries.

A couple of weeks later, I was shopping at a local store when I noticed an older woman in a wheel chair. Her face was drawn. Her mouth was frowning. She was raising her voice to the clerk. She seemed angry about something. The Lord opened my eyes to see a bitter root in her heart that had grown over the years into a prickly thorn bush. I heard the Lord speak to me. "You could have ended up like that woman, but you chose to forgive."

Forgiveness is the shovel that digs up the root of bitterness. Blessing those who hurt you frees you from the entanglement of offense. The garden of your heart must be tended. Proverbs says:

> *My son, pay attention to what I say; turn your ear to my words. Do not let them out of your sight, keep them within your heart; for they are life to those who find them and health to one's whole body. Above all else, guard your heart, for*

everything you do flows from it.

Proverbs 4:20-23 NIV

People end up with ailments, sickness, and disease because of the unwillingness to forgive. Here is another example.

A young woman came to us for help. She needed healing. Her body was calcifying. As we prayed for her, I felt impressed to ask her about her dad.

"Tell me about your dad," I said.

Her face got red and out of her mouth came. "He's a no-good piece of crap!"

There was no talking to her about forgiveness. Her heart was hard and her whole body was following her heart. She left with a hardened heart and a body that followed suit. The sad thing is that freedom was available, but she chose to remain offended and bitter.

> *For if you forgive others for their transgressions, your heavenly Father will also forgive you. But if you do not forgive others, then your Father will not forgive your transgressions.*

Matthew 6:14-15 NASB

Unforgiveness harms us emotionally, spiritually, and physically. Those who have hurt you are not being tormented by your choice to hold onto offense. You are the one who is being hurt—held captive by chains that open the door to tormenting spirits. (See Matthew 18.) Forgiveness is a choice of your will. It is not a feeling. Your will is stronger than your feelings. As you make the choice to forgive, your feelings will come in line with your choice.

Here is a sample prayer of forgiveness:

> _Father, in the name of Jesus, I choose to forgive _____ whether they deserve it or not, because You forgave me whether I deserved it or not. I release anger, bitterness, revenge, and the pain it caused me. I give it to You. Heal my heart. Remove any bitter root from my life. Wash my emotions and restore hope to my heart. Amen_

Deliverance To Freedom

9

Rules or Relationship

"Come to Me, all who are weary and heavy-laden, and I will give you rest. Take My yoke upon you and learn from Me, for I am gentle and humble in heart, and you will find rest for your souls. For My yoke is easy and My burden is light."

Matthew 11:28-30 NASB

For decades in China, young girls' bones were broken and their feet tightly bound in a painful process that would eventually make them appear more desirable to men, according to historians. Their deformed feet, known as lotus feet, were tucked into embroidered shoes and viewed as delicate and dainty. It was a way to show off their social status. It was, at the time, chic. One study, however, suggests that there was another reason girls were subjected to the practice and it wasn't all about beauty or sex. Research published in the book Bound Feet, Young Hands suggests that some women's feet had been bound at a very young age so they could be trained to sit still for hours and help create textiles and clothing for the family. The type of foot-binding practiced in rural communities was a form of discipline, the book argues. Mothers bound young girls' feet so they would stay still and work with their hands, creating yarn and spinning thread, among other things, which families could use or sell.

Women who bound their daughters' feet had their own interests in controlling the labor of young girls and young women," she said. "We reject the view that women were exempted from work, treasuring their precious bound feet and not economically important. They developed hand skills and worked with their hands throughout their lives."

http://www.huffingtonpost.com/entry / chinese-foot-binding-for-work-in-home us 5920f47fe4b03b485cb20dc8

Foot binding was a horrible, painful tradition in Chinese society. As the article above states, it was possibly done for two reasons: to be more attractive to men, or in rural society, to control and discipline young girls for child labor. Their ability to run and play, to walk freely, to eventually leave their parents' side and explore a world of opportunity was taken away by foot binding. Their lives were relegated to countless hours of weaving, spinning, and creating what others dictated. I believe this was a devilish practice.

Rules or Relationship

It was abolished years ago, but foot binding and controlling spirits come from the same root. Let's explore this principle a bit more.

I lead two ministries, one for global transformation and one for local transformation. The latter is a food ministry. We assist around 500 families a month in our local area. Our purpose is to empower our clients with education and counsel in a safe environment where they can receive physical sustenance as well as power to break out of a poverty structure. As a result, we touch elbows with people most people don't meet. We know the homeless, the addicts, the local witches, the chronically ill, the felons, the elderly on fixed income, the runaways, and those who sleep in their car. Most are appreciative of what we do to help them. We have four part-time paid employees and the rest of the staff are volunteers—approximately twenty of them. I could write a book on the amazing people we touch. I have to hold a firm line with them, however, because they are not accustomed to boundaries, except the boundaries dictated to them by their life circumstance.

I believe order is important. Authority structures are in place for a purpose. But when those structures rule over relationship and become detrimental to those we are trying to help, the person standing in front of me is more important. Today was one of those days when the rules didn't work. A man stood in front of me with one week left before he could get more food. He had come three weeks prior. We allow families to come once a month for a grocery cart of food. Our doors are open once a week for a hot meal, and a few groceries for anyone who comes. But his next monthly appointment was a week out. I knew he had nine people in the household, and from what he told me, they had nothing to eat until the next week. This man entered the facility with a walker. He was fighting a crippling disease. I broke the rules for him. He walked out with enough food to sustain the family until their next appointment.

A few years ago, I hired an assistant director who was very rule-oriented. We told our clients to try to arrive on time for their appointments. A young mother with school children was scheduled to come at 4:00 p.m. She arrived at 4:05 p.m., five minutes late because she had to pick the children up from school prior to coming. She was told by Randy Rules (my name for the former assistant director, fictitious of course) that she missed her appointment time and would have to wait until next month to get food. At another distribution, people were required to wait in line until we had everything ready. One of the older women asked if she could come in to use our rest room. Randy Rules would not let her. The older woman exited the building to return to the line when she wet her clothes. She missed the entire distribution.

Sometimes people live such structured lives that there is no room for freedom. The spirit of control actually controls them, and control is rooted in fear. Randy Rules had to control circumstances and people because he was terrified of losing control. I remember the day he looked at me and said, "It's my way or the highway."

The answer was easy. I had to let Randy go because rules were more important to him than the needs of the people.

Now, this next statement may shock you! *God is not in control.* Yes, He is sovereign, but in that sovereignty, He gave us free will. We don't have to obey Him. We choose to because we trust His wisdom and believe He knows what is best for us. God gave rules in the Old Testament to show us our need for a Savior. He knew we couldn't follow those things to the letter. He made provision for our failures through the implementation of blood sacrifice. He ultimately sent His Son to pay the price for our failure to follow the rules.

I personally can't see my Heavenly Father handing me a list of rules and saying "Follow these, and we'll just see if you make it to heaven." Yet, many churches teach rule following over personal relationship with the Father through Jesus Christ by the power of Holy Spirit. People who are afraid of intimacy attend churches like that. It seems safer to follow a rule rather than open your life to the Creator of the Universe. Fear of intimacy, fear of authority, and past, abusive authority figures can cause us to distance ourselves from legitimate, loving leaders. Following rules seems safer than trusting someone you don't know personally.

Here are a few deceptions propagated by rule following churches:

- If you attend church, you are a good person.
- Working for the church is the same as working for God.
- God is not very approachable, so we will tell you what He says.
- You must follow all rules or God will be angry.

The treadmill of church attendance, working to please an angry God, and rule-following ignores and neglects the opportunity to know a loving God whose boundaries for us are protective, not destructive. We have been given freedom to choose our own way, freedom to submit to human control, freedom to refuse it, freedom to rebel against authority, freedom to seek truth for ourselves. Jesus came to show us the Father.

I don't know Phillip's background, but he was very interested in the character of the Father. He asked Jesus this question:

*Philip said to Him, "Lord, show us the Father
and then we will be satisfied." Jesus said to him,
"Have I been with you for so long a time, and you
do not know Me yet, Philip, nor recognize clearly
who I am? Anyone who has seen Me has seen the
Father. How can you say, "Show us the Father?"*

John 14:8-9

I've been controlled by others. I've experienced abusive leadership structures. Phillip and I have a common interest. What is the Father like? Is He loving and approachable? Is He full of rules to follow or is He willing to gently teach me His ways? Will He kick me out if I mess up, or will He pick me up, heal my wounds, and open His arms to me? The prodigal son story answers all of these questions. (See Luke 15:11-31.) God is not after your behavior; He's after your heart. His boundaries are loving; His standards are high. Jesus fulfilled them all. His righteousness is a gift to us. I can rest from my works and step into His grace and power, living life from the inside out instead of the outside in.

Breaking free from rules and living life relationally is risky. It requires trust. It requires opening your heart to God. Our false concepts of Him sometimes keep us from doing that. Following the rules can keep God at a distance. Trust is gained through relationship. His love casts out fear and frees us from the need to control everything and everyone around us. His love invites us into the exclusive dining room of His Presence and points us to the chair at His table with our name on it. Sit down, relax, daddy's home.

Father, show me who you really are. I confess my

Rules or Relationship

fear to you. I've kept you at a distance because I thought you were mean and harsh. I've tried to control my own life and the lives of others because of fear. You have called me to freedom. I trade in my rules for the safety of your Love. Free me to enjoy life, to explore the possibilities in my heart. Unbind my feet. Teach me how to run through the fields of life with you. I chose relationship over rule following. I want to live the abundant life you came to give. I open my heart to receive a true image of a loving Father. Show me personally who you are. I chose to break out of the bondage of controlling rules and live my life pleasing a Father who loves me unconditionally. Amen

Deliverance To Freedom

10

The Donkey and the Carrot

Sustain me, my God, according to your promise,
and I will live; do not let my hopes be dashed.

Psalm 119:116 NIV

Have you ever felt that you were blocked every way you turned? As if you were the mouse looking for the cheese? You could smell the goal but never reach it. Or how about the donkey following the proverbial carrot? Feeling like the donkey lately? You move, the carrot moves! You move again, the carrot moves again! You see it but it remains elusive. I remember crying out to the Lord about that feeling. There were so many dreams inside me, but I was stuck in a familiar place of frustration. I remember telling the Lord how tired I was of waiting for dreams inside me to become reality.

I was on my bed talking to Jesus about how long I had been waiting to see some kind of fulfillment. It was a prayer filled with frustration. I heard Him gently and quietly speak to my heart, "You're my lady in waiting."

It wasn't the answer I anticipated or wanted. In a somewhat irritated voice, I asked, "What is that?"

I decided to research it. I knew it had something to do with serving a King. This was what I found:

> *"For a young woman of noble birth who wished to be at the center of court life, an appointment as Lady-in-Waiting to a princess, duchess or queen was highly coveted. To be selected as a Lady-in-Waiting was considered a mark of high social standing and an honor for the family. These ladies were not servants, but more like companions. They were mostly unpaid. After all, it was a privilege to be chosen."*
>
> https://e-royalty.com/articles/
>
> so-you-want-to-be-a-lady-in-waiting/

After researching lady-in-waiting, I realized I had been invited to an honored place of companionship, a place of intimacy with God. It's not just an invitation to me, but to all who hunger for His Presence. We can wait on the Lord in worship, while we wait for His timing in our lives. I then ran into this scripture:

> *Better is one day in your courts than a thousand elsewhere; I would rather be a doorkeeper in the house of my God than dwell in the tents of the wicked. For the LORD God is a sun and shield; the LORD bestows favor and honor; no good thing does he withhold from those whose walk is blameless.*
>
> Psalm 84-10-11

After reading that scripture, the invitation became clear, the

Lord was honoring me with an invitation to His court, to walk and talk with Him, to dress Him in worship, to show honor to my King. I began to focus more on waiting upon Him, instead of waiting for Him to give me what I wanted. Sometime later, I was leading a prayer meeting in an unfamiliar setting. A man I didn't know came up to me and said he had a word from the Lord for me. I was totally shocked when he said, "The Lord says, you are going to get the carrot!"

I stood there with my mouth open, staring at the man who knew nothing about my prayers concerning the donkey and the elusive carrot, but obediently gave me the word. I'm sure he wrestled with giving it. It had to sound strange to him, but he trusted the Lord's voice. Through God's obedient messenger, I was assured that the carrot, representing the fulfillment of all God had spoken to me, was mine.

Yet, there is more to this story.

A few weeks later, one of my friends brought me a small box. She had purchased a piece of jewelry for me. As she gave it to me, she said, "I know this is a strange gift, but I saw it and thought of you."

I opened the box. Inside was a pin—a beautiful, sparkling, orange and green carrot pin! I wore it for a season, but the message of the pin remains with me forever. It presently sits in my jewelry case. It has no power of its own, of course, but carries a powerful message of hope into my life when I need it.

I was still in a season of waiting, but I had my word from God and my carrot pin to remind me of the faithfulness of God. Circumstances began to change and yet my heart grew stronger as my relationship with my Lord grew deeper. During this period, I had to spend a lot of time with God; He was my lifeline, my hope, and my future.

I wanted to run away from my problems; most of them were internal issues from a rejected past and doubts about my worth. I felt trapped in a labyrinth of self-rejection. I was blinded to the truth of my own identity. Even in my unhealed state, the gifts God had given me from birth were operating. I have a seer gift. I was sitting before the Lord when I saw in my spirit a picture of what I had been feeling. It was a maze, a series of walled cubicles with doors leading to nowhere. A maze is difficult to maneuver, and finding a way out can be exhausting. A maze is defined in dictionary.com as:

> *A confusing network of intercommunicating paths or passages; labyrinth, any complex system or arrangement that causes bewilderment, confusion, or perplexity: a state of bewilderment or confusion.*

http://www.dictionary.com/browse/maze

That definition was exactly how I felt. I asked the Lord to tell me what to do to get out of this maze of bewilderment and confusion. He said, "Look up! There is no lid on your life. You can go as high in me as you want to go. I've given you wings to fly above this thing. Learn to use them. "

Indeed, there was no lid on the maze. I chose to look up, instead of staring at the walls around me, the hemmed in places, the impossible circumstances, the isolation. I cried out, "Teach me to fly!"

Circumstances can be so deceptive. We can be controlled by

them or find the way out. There is a way. He is the Way!

> *Forget the former things; do not dwell on the past.*
> *See, I am doing a new thing! Now it springs up;*
> *do you not perceive it? I am making a way in the*
> *wilderness and streams in the wasteland.*

> Isaiah 43:18-19 NIV

I stopped focusing on the perceived maze and became amazed at the power and glory of my Father God. I was not alone in my pain and frustration. He was walking this road with me. He was holding my hand as we journeyed through the wilderness of deceptive perception. He was teaching me to fly above it all, seeing life from His perspective, viewing the distant horizon of fulfilled dreams with hope, and waiting on Him in worship.

In my process of waiting, I came to love this scripture:

> *Therefore I am now going to allure her; I will lead*
> *her into the wilderness and speak tenderly to her.*
> *There I will give her back her vineyards, and will*
> *make the Valley of Achor a door of hope. There*
> *she will respond as in the days of her youth, as in*
> *the day she came up out of Egypt.*

> Hosea 2:14-15

The allure of God is greater than the gravity of hopelessness that seeks to attach us to the earth and its problems. The law of life in Christ Jesus is greater than the law of sin and death. (See Romans 8:1-2). The law of lift is a greater law than the law of gravity; otherwise, airplanes could not fly. In the same way, the law of life can lift you above the gravity of your circumstances. It's much easier to conquer what has been sent to conquer you, if you see it from God's perspective. Nothing is too difficult for Him.

The valley of Achor was a valley of trouble. In that valley, Israel was defeated in the quest for the city of Ai, because of the sin of Achan. Christiananswers.net describes the Valley of Achor:

> *This was the name of a valley near Jericho, so named because of the trouble which the sin of Achan caused Israel (Joshua 7:24, 26)The expression "valley of Achor" probably became proverbial for that which caused trouble, and when Isaiah (Isaiah 65:10) refers to it, he uses it in this sense: "The valley of Achor, a place for herds to lie down in;" i.e., that which had been a source of calamity would become a source of blessing. Hosea also (Hos. 2:15) uses the expression in the same sense: "The valley of Achor for a door of hope;" i.e., trouble would be turned into joy, despair into hope.*
>
> http://www.christiananswers.net/dictionary/
>
> achor.html

I found the door of hope in my valley of trouble. You can too! Looking at the circumstances keeps you in the maze of confusion, trying to find a way out with limited mobility and understanding. The lid on your maze is off. He is the glory and the lifter of your head.

> *O LORD, how my adversaries have increased! Many are rising up against me. Many are saying*

of my soul, "There is no deliverance for him in God." Selah. But You, O LORD, are a shield about me, My glory, and the One who lifts my head. I was crying to the LORD with my voice, And He answered me from His holy mountain. Selah.

Psalm 3:1-4 NASB

Don't stay in your maze. Be amazed by your God. He is for you. He is the door, the way out of trouble and the way into abundant life. Give Him the reins of your life. Trust Him. Learn to live out of His strength.

"Do you not know? Have you not heard? The Everlasting God, the LORD, the Creator of the ends of the earth Does not become weary or tired. His understanding is inscrutable. He gives strength to the weary, And to him who lacks might He increases power. Though youths grow weary and tired, And vigorous young men stumble badly, Yet those who wait for the LORD Will gain new strength; They will mount up with wings like eagles, They will run and not get tired, They will walk and not become weary."

Isaiah 40:28-31 NASB

Father, in the name of Jesus, I confess my inability to overcome what has been sent to destroy me. You are my glory and the lifter of my head. Put your hand under my chin, lift my eyes toward the heavens. Turn my vision from my problems to see your hand of power reaching out to me. My faith has been weak, but you are strong. I say "yes" to your invitation to learn to fly above my circumstances. I have exhausted my ability; I now step into yours. You are my door of hope. I knock on it now. It opens and I walk through it. Open my eyes to see beyond today. We pass through these valleys. We don't have to live in them. Your Presence changes it all. Amen

From the Psalms:

How blessed is the man whose strength is in You,

In whose heart are the highways to Zion!

Passing through the valley of Baca they make it a spring;

The early rain also covers it with blessings.

They go from strength to strength,

Every one of them appears before God in Zion.

O LORD God of hosts, hear my prayer; Give ear, O God of Jacob! Selah.

Behold our shield, O God,

And look upon the face of Your anointed.

Psalm 84:5-9 NASB

11

Death is Not Your Deliverer!

Remember the word to Your servant, In which You have made me hope. This is my comfort in my affliction, that Your word has revived me.

Psalm 119:49-50 NASB

I've known a few people in my life who chose death as a way out of their pain. Many have been the victim of someone else's wrong choices. They have endured sexual and emotional abuse, abandonment, beatings, drug culture, starvation, slavery, homelessness, bullying, tragedy. The pain of a life filled with trauma can be more than a person can bear. Death offers its deceptive solace to all, masking as the deliverer from unbearable pain and torment. There is a better answer.

Hosea 4:6 says, *"My people are destroyed for lack of knowledge..."* How much of *"all knowledge"* do you possess? Without the wisdom and counsel of an all-knowing God, we are limited in our understanding of how to help those struggling to survive their physical and emotional pain. Help is available. I believe the Lord is standing, waiting, for the troubled, the dying, the outcasts, the broken to come to Him for help. We can point the way to that path of life.

> *"For I will restore you to health And I will heal you of your wounds," declares the LORD, "Because they have called you an outcast, saying: 'It is Zion; no one cares for her.'"*
>
> Jeremiah 30:17 NASB

If all you have known is rejection and trauma, your experience can block the entrance of light and truth. I've seen prayer open a heart that had previously been closed to the Lord's healing power. Some who have come to me for help have asked this question. "If God loves me so much, where was He when those terrible things happened to me?" I'm going to attempt to answer that question. I don't believe everything happens for a reason. That is not Biblical. We do live in a fallen world with an enemy who is out to kill, steal, and destroy. He hates God, and we are made in God's image, created to declare His glory, to display His character and hope to a lost world, to rule and reign with Him bringing heaven's purposes into our realm of authority. Satan wants to destroy that purpose and prolong his own fate.

He is a lion seeking someone to devour.

> *"Be alert and of sober mind. Your enemy the devil prowls around like a roaring lion looking for someone to devour."*
>
> 1 Peter 5:8 NIV

The enemy is attempting to destroy all of us in one way or another. If he cannot get us to commit suicide, he will tempt us with the drugs of sorcery, the seduction of illegitimate sexual activity,

94

the spirit of mammon, the spirit of control, and the list goes on. Another ploy he uses is accusation against God. If we believe God could have rescued us, but didn't, a wall of offense goes up against the only One who can set us free. We have to understand, God is not a controller. He will not step in without your permission or invitation. I believe He is responsible to protect what he owns. He has given us free will to choose our own way. When we chose to walk away from Him, we distance ourselves from His protection.

Psalms 91:1-6 says it this way: *"He who dwells in the shelter of the Most High will abide in the shadow of the Almighty. I will say to the Lord, 'My refuge and my fortress, my God, in whom I trust.'"* For he will deliver you from the snare of the fowler and from the deadly pestilence. He will cover you with his pinions, and under his wings you will find refuge; his faithfulness is a shield and buckler. You will not fear the terror of the night, nor the arrow that flies by day, nor the pestilence that stalks in darkness, nor the destruction that wastes at noonday." Psalms

He is a shelter, but we can choose to come under that shelter or stay out in the rain of circumstance. I cannot blame God for the traumatic things that have happened to me. I have been the victim of someone else's wrong choices. That's not God's fault. The person who hurt me made a choice of his own free will that adversely affected me. I'm not angry with God about that. I'm angry at the choices he made; I'm angry at the ignorance that destroys us; I'm angry at the walls we put up that keep us entrapped in a place we could escape from. It's okay to be angry. Ephesians 4:26 (AMP) says, *"Be angry [at sin—at immorality, at injustice, at ungodly behavior], Yet do not sin; do not let your anger [cause you shame, nor allow it to] last until the sun goes down."*

Jesus is the door to healing. All the counseling in the world will not erase a traumatic memory. Only Jesus can neutralize it with His Presence.

I know the healing Presence of the Lord in my own life. My brother passed away in 1970. I was pregnant with our son when it happened. He and his girlfriend were driving on a country road when his vehicle crossed the line and hit another vehicle with two sisters in it. My brother's girlfriend was killed instantly. My brother was taken to a local hospital with severe head injuries. My Mom and Dad's next-door neighbor showed up at our house banging on the door around 2:00 a.m. We were awakened with the news of the accident. I remember calling my mother-in-law to come over and watch our two-year-old daughter so we could go to the hospital.

I remember riding up in the hospital's elevator, still in shock from being awakened with the news of my brother's accident. A foreboding came over me; I was sick at my stomach. The baby in my womb was moving around as if struggling for a better position. The elevator doors opened. We were immediately hit with the news of the severity of his injuries. I heard a person say, "He's not going to make it. They can't deal with it here, so they are going to take him by ambulance to a larger hospital." I remember the loneliness of that moment, the loss of hope, the trauma of possibly losing my only brother. I don't remember leaving the hospital or getting into the car. I do remember being a part of the caravan of cars following the ambulance to the bigger hospital. About halfway there, the ambulance pulled off the highway. My brother had passed away. He was only nineteen.

I carried the trauma of that memory for years. The echo of the devastating words seemed to be recorded in my brain. The replay button was stuck and replayed the bad news over and over. The pain of that memory was relived multitudes of times. I remember asking the Lord, "Why didn't you take me? He's the only son. There are four of us girls. You could have taken me. Where were you? I don't understand. He was only nineteen."

It took some time to recover. Our son was born five months later. He carries my brother's name. Mom and dad grieved over their loss as did we. We eventually moved on with life, still carrying the scars of trauma. Several years later, I came into an awareness of the power of God to heal traumatic memories. I was encouraged to ask Jesus to come into that memory. In prayer, I invited His Presence to come. I could picture Him standing in the hallway of the hospital when we stepped off the elevator. When we heard the voice spewing bad news, Jesus put His cloak over me and held me in His arms. When the ambulance pulled over and my brother passed away, Jesus spoke and said, "He's with me!"

The Presence of Jesus healed my heart, removed the trauma, and reassured me that my brother is in heaven. I've invited Jesus into other traumatic memories. He is the same yesterday, today, and forever. He is not limited by time or space. Why do we limit what He can do in the lives of those who come to Him?

Just two weeks ago, we were praying with a woman who had been abandoned at birth, placed in an orphanage, and left with little human contact or comfort. While praying for her, she saw a picture of herself as a baby crying in her bed at the orphanage. No one came to comfort her. She was instructed to invite Jesus into that picture. She could see Him reaching for her, picking her up, and giving the comfort she needed. She received an emotional healing that day. I've seen her since that time and she is more secure in the love of God than she was prior to that experience. Our soul is like a camera; our memory is the picture the soul's camera took. Jesus should be in every family picture.

I know from personal and ministry experience the healing power of Jesus. It's never too late to ask Him into your past. You can step into your future without the pain of yesterday. He is real. His principles are not stuck in a dusty book on a coffee table. They are living, active, and able to penetrate the darkness with a holy invasion of His love.

That is why I expose the deceptive false deliverer called suicide. There is hope and healing for those who turn to Jesus. Holy Spirit is the true Deliverer. He does not want us to fail or fall. It's his job through Jesus death, burial, and resurrection to present us holy and blameless before the throne of God.

> *And although you were formerly alienated and hostile in mind, engaged in evil deeds, yet He has now reconciled you in His fleshly body through death, in order to present you before Him holy and blameless and beyond reproach*

> Colossians 1:21-22 NASB

One of the first gifts of the Spirit I operated in was a rescue of someone who was considering suicide. We were in a large church. I was new to the gifts of the Spirit and afraid to step out in a public arena, but the Lord wouldn't leave me alone. I stepped out, made my way to the front and told the pastor in charge that I thought I had a word for someone there. He gave me the microphone. Trembling, I spoke the word He gave me. "There is someone here who feels rejected, not wanted, not valued. Your biological parents gave you up and you were adopted by another family. The Lord wants you to know, that not only did they adopt you, but He has also adopted you into His family. You are important to Him. He has a plan and purpose for your life that is bigger than you can see right now. The scripture I have for you is Romans 8:15 NASB: *"For you have not received a spirit of slavery leading to fear again, but you have received a spirit of adoption as sons by which we cry out, Abba! Father!"* You are His son. He loves you."

I handed the microphone back to the pastor, walked to my seat as quickly as I could, sat down, and listened to the rest of the service. All the while I was feeling very self-aware, thinking I had interrupted the service unnecessarily. After the service was over, a man came up to me. He said, "That word was for me. I was going to kill myself tonight. I came to this service to give God one more chance to show me His love. Thank you for telling me, He loves me and has a purpose for my life." Several of us surrounded that man and prayed for the spirit of suicide to leave him. He found help in the body of Christ.

Why did my brother die in that accident? I could continue to ask that question, or I can hold it until I see God face to face. I understand more now than I did then. I have had to overcome regret at my spiritual immaturity during that season of my life. If I knew then what I know now, perhaps he would still be alive today. That's a question that remains unanswered.

Here's another true story. I was much younger, fifth grade if I remember correctly. We sat at desks designed for two students. I sat on the left, she sat on the right, my best friend and seat partner. I remember telling her about Jesus on the playground during recess. We played together, and her little brother who was in first grade played with us too.

It was a very cold January with ice and snow on the ground. We had been out of school because of it. I remember waking up and running into the kitchen to see if we were having school that day. Mom had a strange look on her face. "What's wrong mom? I asked." It was then she told me about the fire. My friend and her little brother had died in the fire that consumed their house. They were buried in an old cemetery not far from our house. I went to the funeral, returned to school, and sat at the desk by myself. Her books were still on the shelves below mine.

Years later, I decided to look for their graves. I found them in an old cemetery that had been built by slaves. It was surrounded by a wall of stones, with a gated entrance. I drove my car up the dusty gravel driveway. I parked it along the grass and walked around the graves until I found theirs. They were placed right under the flag pole in the center. Standing over their grave stones, I pondered their short lives. I asked the Lord about the unfairness of it all. "Lord," I said, "It seems very unfair that their lives were cut so short. I have lived many years longer than they did. You are a God of restoration. How can you restore the years they lost? I don't understand."

I heard Him speak these words to me. "Would it be all right with you if they returned and lived on the earth with me a thousand years during my millennial reign? Is that enough restoration for you?"

I knew the Lord had spoken. He is a God of restoration. It is not His will for us to experience death, disease, war, poverty, or trauma. We live in a fallen world. But we have a God who restores, heals, and delivers. He retrieved the keys of death, hell, and the grave. He is Life. Choose to live and declare His glory.

Father, forgive me for turning to death as my deliverer. You are the one who gives life, who restores what has been stolen. I have lived too many years in regret and sorrow. Heal my heart. Give me a new picture of the traumatic events in my life with you in them. Your Presence is healing. Your grace is carrying me, and abundant life awaits. Suicide is not the answer. Death is our enemy. You have defeated it by your resurrection.

For He must reign until He has put all His enemies under His feet. The last enemy that will be abolished is death.

I Corinthians 15:25-26 NASB

Deliverance To Freedom

12

Bloodline Iniquity and Curses

In chapter 11, we talked about our enemy who is like a lion looking for someone to devour. If he cannot reach you through open doors of sin or transgression, he will look for something in your bloodline. Sin is missing the mark; transgression is crossing a boundary. Iniquity is generational sin.

In 1999, I was invited to be part of a team praying at twelve sites from the east to the west coast of America. We had been on the road for several days and had completed our assignment at eleven sites and were headed to the twelfth. I heard the enemy say, "If you finish this assignment, I'm going to kill your son." I told the team about the threat. We prayed against it and decreed Proverbs 14:26 NIV over my two sons and daughter.

> *Whoever fears the LORD has a secure fortress,*
> *and for their children it will be a refuge."*

I finished the assignment trusting the Lord to be a refuge for my children.

About two weeks later, one of my sons was getting out of his vehicle on the streets of Kansas City with a group of people. It was right before dark. The group entered a house while my son locked the car. A man with a gun approached him, pointed it at his chest and asked for his billfold. He refused to give it to him. Once again, the robber demanded my son's billfold. He again refused and moved toward the gunman trying to stop him. This time the gunman pointed the gun at my son and attempted to shoot him in the stomach. The bullet hit his belt buckle bounced off and pierced through his leg. The gunman fled. My son told me later that an unknown man helped him into the house where his friends had gathered. Then that man mysteriously disappeared. We now believe that unknown man was an angel.

The bullet that pierced Scott's leg missed an artery by a quarter of an inch. The belt buckle he was wearing was an Electric Light Orchestra belt buckle with the initials, ELO, engraved on it. Eventually, the gunman was caught from a police lineup and Scott recovered. I thanked the Lord for saving my son. I realized if the bullet had not bounced off the belt buckle, he could have been killed. I asked the Lord about that belt buckle. "Lord, you used that belt buckle to deflect that bullet. I'm sure you were there." He spoke to me and said, "Yes, add HIM to it." I didn't understand at first. Then I wrote out *E-L-O-H-I-M*. Elohim!

Elohim was there. He protected my son! I explored that name and found greater understanding of the One I serve, the One who is faithful and true.

Question: "What is the meaning of the word Elohim?

Answer: Elohim is a Hebrew word that denotes "God" or "god." It is one of the most common names for God in the Old Testament, starting in the very first verse: *"In the beginning [Elohim] created the heavens and the earth"* (Genesis 1:1). The name Elohim occurs over 2,500 times in the Tanakh.

The basic meaning behind the name Elohim is one of strength or power of effect. Elohim is the infinite, all-powerful God who shows by His works that He is the creator, sustainer, and supreme judge of the world. "Bring to an end the violence of the wicked and make the righteous secure—you, the righteous [Elohim] who probes minds and hearts" (Psalm 7:9). (https://www.gotquestions.org/meaning-of-Elohim.html)

God intervened and saved my son from the threat of the enemy. Elohim was a refuge for my child. A couple of weeks later, Ryan, our second son was getting off work late at night and stopped by a convenience store to make a purchase. A man with a gun pointed it at him and told him to lay face down on the floor. The gunman robbed the clerk and fled. Scott was home in bed asleep, woke up suddenly, knew his brother was in danger, and prayed for his safety.

Needless to say, these two incidents within two weeks of each other got my attention. Both of the gunmen were black. I asked Chuck Pierce why these two robbers had access to my sons. I knew the enemy was trying to destroy them, but what was the open door. Chuck said, "Look for racism in the bloodline."

I called my mother and asked her if we had racism in our bloodline. "Yes," she said. "Our ancestors were slave owners a few generations back." That was the open door the enemy used against us. If he can't get you through known sin or transgression, he will search your bloodline for the legal right to bring destruction against you. But God intervened.

> *My God is my rock, in whom I take refuge, my shield and the horn of my salvation. He is my stronghold, my refuge and my savior—from*

violent people you save me. I called to the LORD, who is worthy of praise, and have been saved from my enemies.

2 Samuel 22:3-4 NIV

We repented for the racism in our bloodline. The power of that iniquity was broken and the door of access to our family was shut. The principle of repenting for the sins of the previous generations is exampled by Nehemiah. He repented for the sins of his fathers:

> *Then I said: "LORD, the God of heaven, the great and awesome God, who keeps his covenant of love with those who love him and keep his commandments, let your ear be attentive and your eyes open to hear the prayer your servant is praying before you day and night for your servants, the people of Israel. I confess the sins we Israelites, including myself and my father's family, have committed against you. We have acted very wickedly toward you. We have not obeyed the commands, decrees and laws you gave your servant Moses."*

Nehemiah 1:5-7 NIV

Moses asked forgiveness for the sins of the generations:

The LORD is slow to anger, abounding in love and forgiving sin and rebellion. Yet he does not leave the guilty unpunished; he punishes the children for the sin of the parents to the third and fourth generation. In accordance with your great love, forgive the sin of these people, just as you have pardoned them from the time they left Egypt until now.

The sin of Jeroboam and his house, his bloodline, caused their destruction.

Even after this, Jeroboam did not change his evil ways, but once more appointed priests for the high places from all sorts of people. Anyone who wanted to become a priest he consecrated for the high places. This was the sin of the house of Jeroboam that led to its downfall and to its destruction from the face of the earth.

Yes, Jesus became a curse for us when he hung on that cross. (See Galatians 3:13). But we have to apply and enforce that victory. Bloodline curses exist today. They will not be totally wiped away until the restoration of all things.

> *"No longer will there be any curse. The throne of God and of the Lamb will be in the city, and his servants will serve him."*
>
> Revelation 22:3 NIV

Curses still exist today. We can be impacted by them. Why are we not breaking out of lack? Why is sickness or disease attacking our family? Why is divorce a reoccurring issue? The answer could be that a curse is in operation. We break those curses through repentance. The devil is a legalist. He demands the right to hinder or destroy us when he can find access through our bloodline.

> *Like a sparrow in its flitting, like a swallow in its flying, So a curse without cause does not alight.*
>
> Proverbs 26:2

Robert Henderson states in his blog:

> *Some of the things the devil uses to steal our*

*God-ordained life are these curses. My definition
for a curse is "a spiritual force used by the devil
to sabotage success and futures." When a curse
is operating people are filled with frustration
because they can never quite reach what they
intuitively know they were created for. But the
answer is not to stop dreaming. The answer is to
get the curse removed and their powers broken
so dreams are not sabotaged and can come true.
Life without dreams is not worth living. We were
built by God to dream.*

*The key to dealing with adverse forces that resist
and work against us is to remove their legal rights.
Everything is legal in the spirit realm. Curses
can only operate from a legal position. Proverbs,
chapter 26, verse 2, gives us some insight into the
operation of curses: "Like a flitting sparrow, like a
flying swallow, so a curse without cause shall not
alight" (Proverbs 26:2).*

*Curses must have a cause or a legal right to land.
They cannot land just anywhere. They have to
find a cause or legal reason to put their feet down.
To be able to undo or remove a curse and stop
its power against us we must remove the legal
reason it has found to land and operate. When
this occurs, the limitations imposed by the devil
legally are removed.*

Bloodline Iniquity and Curses

https://www.destinyimage.com/blogs/news/robert-henderson-breaking-curses-in-the-courts-of-heaven

Curses exist today. Unbeknownst to me, I was being held back by one. I was in a meeting with Barbara Yoder in Ann Arbor, Michigan, along with a team from *Glory of Zion* to deal with an issue affecting the United States. I had checked into the hotel prior to the gathering. My room was on the third floor, room 331. The thermostat wouldn't work. I called the desk and was moved to a different room on the second floor.

When I settled into the new room, I heard the Lord say, "Look up the room number you just left in the Strong's." I found 331 in the Greek section. I read the word, anathema. It was a curse pronounced by religious authority. I heard the Lord say, "I'm releasing you from a curse spoken against you by someone with ecclesiastical authority. When you go to that gathering tonight, ask Barbara Yoder to touch your head. I will release you from that curse."

I knew there was a lid on my life, that something was hindering me from getting where I was intended to go. A curse had been released against me that needed to be broken. I was pretty sure I knew who had spoken against me, but that was not as important as breaking out of it. I arrived at the meeting, sat in the second row, and waited for the Lord to direct me. The worship time was wonderful; prophetic declarations were coming forth. I had been on the stage giving prophetic utterance.

When worship was almost over, I heard the Lord say, "Go up on the stage and ask Barbara to touch your head. I want to break that curse." I was sitting in the second row behind well-known leaders. I did not want to get out of my seat, walk to the stage, and

109

be the focus of everyone there. "Lord, now?"

He replied, "Yes, now."

I got out of my seat, walked up on the stage toward Barbara. She thought I had another prophetic word and started to hand me the microphone. I shook my head, and said, "Touch me on the forehead." She did, and I flew half way across the stage, ending up on my face, weeping from the core of my being. This was not the way I wanted to be delivered from a curse. There I was in the sight of everyone, feeling the effects of breaking out from under a curse, crying from its release. Mary Audrey Raycroft, who works with Barbara, came up on the stage, took my head into her lap, and allowed me to have some shelter from the eyes of the audience.

I finally was helped off the stage. I knew that curse was broken. My life began to change after that. Doors opened that had previous been closed. Breakthroughs started coming in many areas. I've shared this story with many people, who have asked me to break ecclesiastical curses off of them. Many people wonder why things just don't come together for them, why they are not recognized or received for who they are. Ask the Lord to show you if a curse is operating against you.

The bloodline curse that was operating against our family had to be removed. It was done through repentance for the sins of the fathers. The ecclesiastical curse was broken by someone who had a breaker anointing to remove it. Allow the Lord to show you where you have been hindered by bloodline curses. The Lord has given you overcoming power to defeat your enemies. What you have conquered, you have authority over.

This book is by no means a complete picture of deliverance from darkness, but it is intended to start you on the journey to freedom. The Freedom Map addendum is for your personal use and created to assist you in setting others free.

The connection between freedom, spiritual cleansing, and the release of the glory is clear.

> *When the Lord has washed away the filth of the daughters of Zion and purged the bloodshed of Jerusalem from her midst, by the spirit of judgment and the spirit of burning, then the LORD will create over the whole area of Mount Zion and over her assemblies a cloud by day, even smoke, and the brightness of a flaming fire by night; for over all the glory will be a canopy. There will be a shelter to give shade from the heat by day, and refuge and protection from the storm and the rain.*
>
> Isaiah 4:4-6

Deliverance To Freedom

13

Freedom Map - The Way Out!

This Freedom Map was created to assist you in praying for those desiring freedom. When consulting a map, there is a destination in mind. Our destination is freedom. You will want to use your GPS, God's Positioning System, revelation from Holy Spirit to navigate through unfamiliar territory. The gifts of the Spirit will be in operation giving words of knowledge, words of wisdom, and prophetic insight, to assist in breaking through barriers of spiritual resistance.

Before walking through these prayers with someone else, it would be wise for you to pray through them, allowing the Holy Spirit to reveal areas of your life that require cleansing. When praying for someone else, I do not recommend a one-on-one approach. It is wise to have two people working together for greater authority, accountability, and spiritual perception. Before praying for another person, make sure they are determined to wholly follow the Lord. Sometimes a person just wants relief from the guilt and torment of a sinful life, rather than completely turning to the Lord. Invite Holy Spirit to be the Deliverer. Ask Him to free the person you are praying for. Remember you are the instrument God is using; He is doing the work through you. It is a good practice to pray for Holy Spirit's help in the presence of the one you are ministering to, so they look to Him for their freedom, and don't become dependent on you or your ministry.

Because you are invading the enemy's territory with the power of God, pray a prayer of protection over your life, your family, and everything that you steward. You are in covenant with God through Jesus Christ. His blood cleanses and protects you. But decreeing that into place prior to a ministry session to set others free, is wisdom.

Sample prayer of protection:

> *Father, in the name of Jesus, I ask You to protect me, my family, my relationships, and possessions from evil. I thank You that the blood of Jesus is on the doorposts of our household and we are safe, free from any attacks of the enemy. You are our strong tower; we dwell in You, safe from harm or backlash. You have given us stewardship over possessions, land, and ministry. We decree that no evil will prosper against us or enter our territory. We live, and move, and have our dwelling place in You. Thank you for your protection. Amen*

Another word of caution is to be discerning about who you minister to. I recently had a request to pray for someone I did not know, who was extremely tormented by evil spirits. I agreed to pray for this person, not realizing it was a set-up to bring contention and accusation. The instruction given to him following ministry was not followed, nor did he fight for himself. I learned from the experience and have implemented an application process that yields more information about the client. Also, remember: You do not have to pray for everyone who requests it.

> _"I am sending you out like sheep among wolves. Therefore, be as shrewd as snakes and as innocent as doves."_
>
> Matthew 10:16 NIV

Now that I have established a few guidelines, let's look towards the destination of freedom for ourselves and others. These following prayers are for those who already know the Lord. If the person is not "born again", lead them in a prayer to receive Jesus as Lord and Savior. Then proceed with the prayers for freedom. Remember to have the person you are praying for pray these prayers out loud. It is important that they hear their own voice decreeing these prayers of salvation and renunciation. This will build faith in them for their release from bondage.

> _So faith comes from hearing, and hearing by the word of Christ._
>
> Romans 10:17 NASB

Sample Prayer for Salvation:

> _Father God, in the name of Jesus, I ask forgiveness for my sins. I accept You as my Savior and Lord. I know Your blood was shed to save me. I accept Your sacrifice for my sins, transgressions, and iniquity. Please come live in my heart; bring me into the abundant life You already purposed for me. Wash me clean of my past; set my feet on the_

path of life. I give myself completely to You, spirit,
soul, and body. Amen

OPEN DOORS OF ACCESS TO OUR ENEMY:

We will look at ten doors of access the enemy uses to gain a foothold in a person's life. These doors of access are opened through disobedience to God's Word knowingly or unknowingly. Because we are dealing with a thief whose goal is to steal, kill, and destroy, these doors of access must be closed by us through confession and repentance before the Lord, followed by removing the evil spirits that entered through those doors. Because their legal right of access has been taken away, they have no alternative but to leave.

> *So Jesus said again, "I assure you and most*
> *solemnly say to you, I am the Door for the sheep*
> *[leading to life]. All who came before Me [as false*
> *messiahs and self-appointed leaders] are thieves*
> *and robbers, but the [true] sheep did not hear*
> *them. I am the Door; anyone who enters through*
> *Me will be saved [and will live forever], and will*
> *go in and out [freely], and find pasture (spiritual*
> *security). The thief comes only in order to steal*
> *and kill and destroy. I came that they may have*
> *and enjoy life, and have it in abundance [to the*
> *full, till it overflows]."*

John 10:7-10 AMP

1. UNCONFESSED SIN

Key Scripture

"Therefore, confess your sins to one another

[your false steps, your offenses], and pray for one another, that you may be healed and restored. The heartfelt and persistent prayer of a righteous man (believer) can accomplish much [when put into action and made effective by God—it is dynamic and can have tremendous power]."

James 5:16 AMP

Repentance is the key to freedom from the effects of sin. The enemy looks for a legal right to enter a person's life. Sin gives him access. Once the enemy has entered, he will begin to operate from that place until the sin is confessed and repented of. Satan and his cohorts traffic in darkness; confession and repentance take away their power. The light (confession) exposes them and the repentance removes their legal right to be there. Remember Holy Spirit is the deliverer; He knows what is in the heart of each person. From experience, I have learned that deception can cover up what is in the heart of a person, keeping them from seeing or hearing clearly, so always ask Holy Spirit to reveal any unconfessed sin to the person you are praying for.

Sample prayer of repentance:

"Father, in the name of Jesus, I confess the sin of _____. I sinned against You and Your Word. Please forgive me; cleanse my heart from the effects of my disobedience. I choose to follow You fully from this day forward. Give me your grace to remain in right standing with You. Thank You for the blood of Jesus that cleanses me from sin. "

Deliverance To Freedom

Once the prayer of repentance is prayed, you may want to lead the person in commanding certain demonic spirits to leave. This is not a shouting match with the devil, but a simple command with the authority of a believer. The legal right of the enemy to occupy a place of darkness in the person's life has been removed through repentance, so a simple command is all that is needed.

As Holy Spirit brings up sins, continue to lead the person through repentance prayers. Depending on what sin is being confessed, you may have to jump over to another section of this guide to completely free them. For instance, if the unconfessed sin requires the need for forgiveness of others, you would lead them through the forgiveness section. If rash vows have been made, you would lead them in renouncing them.

2. UNFORGIVENESS

Key Scripture

> *Be kind and helpful to one another, tender-hearted [compassionate, understanding], forgiving one another [readily and freely], just as God in Christ also forgave you.*

> Ephesians 4:32 AMP

See also Matthew 18:21-35

Unforgiveness opens the door to bitterness, resentment, anger, hatred, revenge, retaliation, as well as a host of physical diseases. Forgiveness is not given for the benefit of the instigator of the violation, but for the one who was violated. It delivers the captive person from torment, disease, and a plethora of dark spirits whose purpose is to steal peace and inflict torment. Forgiveness is not a feeling, but a choice. The will is stronger than emotion. The power of choice supersedes the power of feeling. Emotion will come into alignment after the person chooses to forgive.

A young woman came for ministry. She was so tormented that she could not sleep, nor could she complete simple tasks. One of the ministers asked her if she was angry at God. (I believe the question was a gift of the Spirit called a Word of Knowledge. God was revealing the source of her torment.)

As her story came gushing out, she admitted her anger toward the Lord. Her fiancé had suddenly dropped dead, two years previous, while they were walking together in a park, making plans for their future together. She held unforgiveness toward God for taking him from her. In reality, it was not God's fault, yet in her heart and mind, she had blamed Him. We led her in a prayer to forgive God, releasing Him from her blame, anger, resentment, and bitterness. After she released her fiancé into the hands of the Lord, letting him go, she was able to think rationally and realize that God was for her, not against her, and that He had plans for her future. With her permission, we commanded the spirit of torment to leave. Her countenance changed as she felt the relief from its grip. The unforgiveness she had carried for two years was gone and so was the mental and emotional torment. She was stuck emotionally and spiritually in a tragic event that held her in its grip.

It is not wise to try to explain why these tragedies happen. I personally don't believe everything happens for a reason, meaning there is a redemptive purpose in it. Some things happen because the enemy finds an open door to kill, steal, and destroy. We may never know the why's of tragedies and traumas, but they can be healed by the Presence of God. The bottom line is: God can be trusted, and He has plans for us that are good and not evil to give us a future and a hope.

> *For I know the plans that I have for you,' declares the Lord, 'plans for welfare and not for calamity to give you a future and a hope.*

Jeremiah 29:11 NASB

Sample prayer of repentance:

> *Father, in the name of Jesus, I choose to forgive ————————-, whether they deserve it or not, because Jesus forgave me when I didn't deserve it. I release to You Lord all bitterness, resentment, revenge, retaliation, hatred, (allow Holy Spirit to speak to the person perhaps bringing up other feelings). I let go of my need to be right in this situation and choose Your righteousness over my rightness.*

Note: If the forgiveness section brings up the need to cut soul ties or break rash vows, you will need to go to that section of prayers to totally remove the bondage.

Continue leading the person through forgiving each one who has harmed or violated them. There may be times when the person you are praying for asks the question, "Where was Jesus when this bad thing happened to me?" That question can only be answered by the Lord. Our response is to ask the Lord to show them where He was in that situation. Because the Lord is not limited by time, He can go back into that trauma or situation and redeem it by giving them a new picture of the painful memory with Him in it. Memory is similar to a video; it will surface during ministry. That painful memory can be healed when Jesus is invited into it.

During ministry to another young woman, a tragic memory surfaced from her childhood. She had been beaten severely by her step-father for a minor offense. He made her remove all her clothes and then proceeded to beat her with a switch that he cut from a tree in the backyard. She remembered the pain, the deep marks on her body from the cruel beating, and the anger he demonstrated toward her. After she released forgiveness to her step-father, which freed her from bitterness and rage, she asked, "Where were You Jesus when this happened to me? Would You give me a new picture of that memory with You in it?"

She invited Jesus to show her what He would have done if He had been there. She pictured Jesus enter into that memory, cover her with a blanket, pick her up in His arms, stop the abuse, and carry her to a safe place where she was loved and protected. After she received the new picture, she still remembered the beating, but Jesus was always there in her memory bank. The trauma was neutralized by the Presence of the Lord.

3. IDOLATRY AND FALSE RELIGION

Key Scriptures

> *For be sure of this: no immoral, impure, or greedy person—for that one is [in effect] an idolater—has any inheritance in the kingdom of Christ and God [for such a person places a higher value on something other than God].*
>
> Ephesians 5:5 AMP

> *And the Lord has sent to you all His servants the prophets again and again, but you have not*

listened nor inclined your ear to hear, saying,
"Turn now everyone from his evil way and
from the evil of your deeds, and dwell on the
land which the Lord has given to you and your
forefathers forever and ever; and do not go after
other gods to serve them and to worship them,
and do not provoke Me to anger with the work of
your hands, and I will do you no harm."

Jeremiah 25:4-6

False Religion

Turning to anyone or anything other than the Lord Himself as the source of life and help can make them an idol. Religion, defined as self-effort, can be a substitute for relationship with God and also become an idol. God reached us because we couldn't reach Him. The gulf was too wide, the way blocked, and no amount of self-effort could bring us back into right relationship with our Creator. False religion puts the responsibility of reaching God back on us. It is arrogant to believe we can please God with our efforts, yet man still creates his own way through religious behaviors that may placate the conscience but always lead to failure. The building of the Tower of Babel in Genesis 11 is a picture of man's effort to build a name for himself and reach into the heavens by building a tower brick by brick. Instead of making bricks (self-effort), we are invited by God's grace through Jesus Christ to be living stones, being built into a spiritual house.

For if God did not spare angels when they sinned,
but cast them into hell and committed them to
pits of darkness, reserved for judgment; and did

not spare the ancient world, but preserved Noah, a preacher of righteousness, with seven others, when He brought a flood upon the world of the ungodly; and if He condemned the cities of Sodom and Gomorrah to destruction by reducing them to ashes, having made them an example to those who would live ungodly lives thereafter;

I Peter 2:4-6

Any religion that removes Jesus as the only way to God — replacing Him or adding to His sacrifice — is at least a dead-end road, and at most a counterfeit for relationship with God. False religions include Mormonism, Jehovah Witness, Christian Science, Unity, Freemasonry, Islam, Hinduism, and New Age. This list is not complete. You will begin to recognize others as they surface in ministry sessions.

Sample Prayer of Repentance for Participating in False Religion:

Father, in the name of Jesus, I confess that I have participated in   (name of false religion) .
I recognize that the sacrifice of Jesus on the cross is the only way to You. Forgive me for opening a wrong door spiritually. I know from John 10 that I must enter through the door, who is Jesus. I remove my name and our family's names from that altar, and I ask for Your blood to cleanse this sin from us. I choose to have no other gods before You. I give back anything I received from that false worship altar, and trade it in for Your grace

in my life and choose to walk with You by the power of your Spirit. Amen

Idolatry

The first of the Ten Commandments described Idolatry well: *"You shall have no other gods before me"* (Exodus 20:3). From the New Testament, Philippians 3:19 is also a good description of idolatry: *"Their end is destruction, their god is their belly, and they glory in their shame, with minds set on earthly things."* (See also Rev 21:8, Psalms 31:6, Leviticus 19:1-4.)

When many of us try to define idolatry, we picture stone statues of birds, animals, or false gods in various forms. Idolatry includes these images, but also includes anything or anyone we turn to as a life source. Recently, a friend shared how the Lord had convicted her of idolatry. When she was overwhelmed, instead of turning to the Lord, she would go shopping, spending money on things she didn't need. When Jesus convicted her of this behavior, she asked forgiveness and fasted shopping for over a month, turning to the Lord instead. After she weaned herself from her shopping idolatry, she was able to restore it to its proper place.

Sample Prayer for Repentance For Idolatry:

Father, in the name of Jesus, I confess that I have looked to things in this world to satisfy my desires, to be a source of life for me. I ask Your forgiveness for turning to _____ instead of You. I choose to make You Lord over every area of my life. I close the door to all idols in my life and open the door to You as my Source of Life. Amen

Ask Holy Spirit to reveal idols in the person's life. Possible idols could include drugs, alcohol, sex, pornography, people, personal performance, fear of man, personal recognition, food, etc.

4. INVOLVEMENT IN THE OCCULT

Key Scripture

> *"When you enter the land which the LORD your God is giving you, you shall not learn to imitate the detestable (repulsive) practices of those nations. There shall not be found among you anyone who makes his son or daughter pass through the fire [as a sacrifice], one who uses divination and fortune-telling, one who practices witchcraft, or one who interprets omens, or a sorcerer, or one who casts a charm or spell, or a medium, or a spiritist, or a necromancer [who seeks the dead]. For everyone who does these things is utterly repulsive to the LORD; and because of these detestable practices the LORD your God is driving them out before you. For these nations which you shall dispossess listen to those who practice witchcraft and to diviners and fortune-tellers, but as for you, the LORD your God has not allowed you to do so."*

> Deuteronomy 18:9-12, 14 AMP

There are two sources of knowledge in the spirit realm. Legitimate spiritual knowledge is through the Word of God, by the power of God's Spirit. Seeking spiritual knowledge from the dark side is forbidden by scripture. We are not to seek witches, psychics, talk to the dead, pray to saints, participate in seances, or seek spiritual power from any other source besides the Lord, His Spirit, and His Word. Witches, warlocks, and psychics do exist in today's world, seducing victims through dark spiritual doors to obtain illegitimate knowledge from illegitimate sources. These doors of access allow the enemy to occupy space in that person's life, using them for his evil agenda. Oppression, depression, religious delusions, unrelenting anxiety, excessive self-pity, destructive thoughts and actions can be a result of occult involvement.

Have you or your family been involved in any of the following areas? (Note: Even *casual* involvement must be repented of.)

- read horoscopes or participated in astrology

- been hypnotized or used hypnotism in any way

- had your fortune told in any way including cards, tea leaves, crystal ball, Ouija board, palm reading, planchette (even casually as a child)

- played occult games such as telepathy, ESP, Dungeons & Dragons, Kabbala

- watched movies involving the occult

- attempted to control or manipulate others

- received a life or reincarnation reading

- possessed occult objects

- owned books or objects of an occult nature such as skulls, pentagram, amulets, talismans, figures of gods, devil masks, witchcraft fantasy books, Mormonism books, Jehovah's Witness material, statues of Saints used for worship. (Deuteronomy 7:26)

- sought psychics for any reason - _or medium_
- ghost hunted and explored haunted houses
- been involved in witchcraft, sorcery, casting of spells, hexes, curses
- taken mind altering drugs such as cocaine, LSD, marijuana, or abused prescription drugs
- practiced transcendental meditation or put your mind in a passive state
- been involved in secret practices or secret fraternities _Job's Daughters   Masonry etc._

Sample Prayer of Repentance from Occult Activity:

_Father, in the name of Jesus, I confess that I have sinned against You and Your Word by participating in ____(specific involvement)____. I ask for Your forgiveness. I give back anything I received from those activities including dark spirits, oppression, spiritual knowledge from wrong sources, and command any door of access to the enemy to be closed. Jesus, You are Lord of my mind, my will, and my emotions. You, by the power of Your Holy Spirit, on the foundation of Your Word, are my only source of spiritual knowledge. In Jesus Name, Amen_

At this point, you would command any occult spirits to leave, or ask the person you are praying for to do so. A partial list of occult spirits is: divination, spiritism, witchcraft, control, rebellion, sorcery, torment, etc.

Note: Ask Holy Spirit to reveal to the person you are praying for, any occult activity that needs to be repented of.)

5. SEXUAL SIN

Key scripture

> *Now the practices of the sinful nature are clearly evident: they are sexual immorality, impurity, sensuality (total irresponsibility, lack of self-control), idolatry, sorcery, hostility, strife, jealousy, fits of anger, disputes, dissensions, factions [that promote heresies], envy, drunkenness, riotous behavior, and other things like these. I warn you beforehand, just as I did previously, that those who practice such things will not inherit the kingdom of God.*
>
> Galatians 5:19-21 AMP

The Bible forbids sexual activity outside of marriage. There is evidence that women contain DNA from every sexual partner they have had. It has long been acknowledged that pieces of our soul are left behind in sexual encounters. Therefore, following repentance, soul ties must be severed. Pornography is harmful to relationships and fills the mind with images that become addictive. It is an act of unfaithfulness toward one's spouse. Homosexuality and lesbianism are also forbidden.

Sample Prayer for Repentance for Sexual Activity Outside of Marriage:

> *Father, in the name of Jesus, I ask Your forgiveness for fornication, adultery, pornography, prostitution, and all forbidden sexual activity*

outside of marriage. I have sinned against You and Your Word, acted in rebellion, and allowed portions of my soul to be captured by another person. Forgive me, Father. I choose to follow Your word and renounce all past unlawful sexual activity. I ask for Your blood to cleanse me from all unrighteousness. I know my body is a temple of Holy Spirit. May I be emptied of all sin and filled with Your grace and mercy.

Unhealthy Soul Ties

The Word of God forbids sexual activity outside of marriage. Our soul can become fractured and broken by illegitimate sexual or emotional ties to another person. In Psalms 23:3 David wrote,

> *He refreshes and restores my soul (life); He leads me in the paths of righteousness for His name's sake.*
>
> Psalm 23:3 AMP

Restoration of the soul begins with repentance and continues as we cut illegitimate ties with previous sexual partners. Many marriages are severely handicapped because both husband and wife have had sexual intercourse with previous partners, leaving parts of themselves behind. Cutting those ties and reclaiming the parts of our soul we left behind through illegitimate sexual activity brings restoration and healing to the fractured soul.

Codependency can also open the door to emotional attachments that can require cutting of emotional soul ties with that person. This can happen with a cult leader, a close friend, or a controlling associate.

Sample Prayer to Cut Sexual Soul Ties:

"Father in the Name of Jesus, I choose to cut a soul tie with <name>. I ask Your forgiveness for illegitimate sexual relationship with that person. I cut my soul free from <name>, and I give back what I gained through that act, including that person's DNA. Restore my fractured soul. Send Your angels to bring back what I lost. "

Sample Prayer to Cut Emotional Soul Ties:

"Father, in the Name of Jesus, I admit an illegitimate emotional attachment to <name>.

I have looked to that person to lead me, to satisfy the empty space in my heart, instead of You. Out of my need, I allowed an emotional attachment to entangle my life and keep me in bondage to their approval. You alone can satisfy me. I ask Your forgiveness for this entanglement and choose to break it now by the power of Your Spirit. I release them and let them go. I give myself to You totally and completely, spirit, soul, and body. Please restore my soul in this area."

6. RASH VOWS

Key Scripture

It is better that you should not vow than that you should vow and not pay.

Ecclesiastes 5:5 NASB

Freedom Map - The Way Out!

Vows are inner decisions or vocalized decrees concerning yourself or others. Rash vows are impulsive, sometimes reckless statements or thoughts originating from frustration or disgust for a person or situation. The problem with rash vows is that we do not have the power to keep them. From experience in ministering to people, I have seen that which they vowed they would never do, become a reality in their lives.

A young woman came to me for ministry. She had fallen into a pattern that had plagued her mother. Her mother was weak willed and had allowed circumstances and people to rule her. She constantly submitted to others demands. This young lady had made a rash statement, a vow, that she would never be like her mother. She would stand up for herself and make her own decisions. The vow she made had no power, and she fell into the same pattern as her mother, allowing others to dictate her life. We led her in a prayer of repentance for making a vow she had no power to keep. Instead of vowing against her mother's weak-willed behavior, she chose to ask the Lord to demonstrate His character through her.

Sample Prayer of Repentance for rash vows:

> *"Father, in the Name of Jesus, I ask Your forgiveness for making a vow that I had no power to keep. I repent for the rash statements I have made. (List them)*

I choose to allow You to live through me. Break the repetitive patterns of behavior in my life and fill me with Your Spirit. I choose the fruits of the Spirit in my life. "

7. Bitter Root Judgments

Key Scripture

See to it that no one falls short of the grace of God
and that no bitter root grows up to cause trouble
and defile many.

Hebrews 12:15 NIV

It probably goes without saying that bitter root judgments arise from a bitter root. This can stem from unmet needs, personal loss, or disappointment. Most people have unfulfilled expectations that have produced disappointment. If disappointment is not dealt with by submitting it to the Lord and allowing Him to wash it out of us, it can grow into hurt, rejection, and unforgiveness toward those whose lives seem to be going better than ours. We can become angry at others because we see them enjoying what we seemingly have missed. We lash out with judgments against them. We want to tear them down because we feel they have somehow taken what could have been ours. We say things like, "Look at her. She thinks she's God's gift to mankind. I heard she's had 3 surgeries just to get her nose fixed." Or, "That guy is President of the company, but you know, his father owns it and gave it to him." Instead of rejoicing over someone else's blessing, we try to find a flaw that gives us the right to release judgment against them.

Those judgments might never be spoken, but they lodge in our hearts and will manifest through our attitudes toward others. They can grow into jealousy and produce the fruit of contention.

Sample Prayer of Repentance for Bitter Root Judgments:

"Father, in the Name of Jesus, I ask Your
forgiveness for allowing my disappointments

to grow into bitterness and judgments against others. Your word tells us to "rejoice with those who rejoice." I have not been willing to do that because I have been comparing my life to theirs, and seeing myself as the one who has been left out of the blessing circle. I didn't feel that You blessed me, so I didn't want them to be blessed either. I tried to take them down from a place of success by the power of my words. Forgive me, Father. I chose to let go of my right to judge. I chose to allow You to wash away my disappointments, and I chose to bless those of whom I have been jealous. You are my source. I let go of my agenda for my life and allow You to take over. My future is in Your hands. I will receive what You have for me and stop trying to get what others have. Thank you, Lord for delivering me from bitterness and judgment."

Note: If there are specific people that you have released judgments against, release them from the curses you have spoken against them and release blessing instead. We cannot be fully blessed until we rejoice in the blessings of others.

8. Trauma

Trauma is injury to the soul and takes up lodging in our memory bank. It grows unless we negate its power by allowing Holy Spirit to give us a new picture of the traumatized memory.

When we are praying for people in this area, they often ask, "Where was God when this happened to me?" Here are a few partial answers:

- We live in a fallen world and are sometimes the victim of other people's choices.

- God is responsible to protect what He fully owns. Were you His when you experienced the trauma?

- Sometimes curses are in operation that need to be broken through bloodline repentance and cleansing.

- We may never know! But because Jesus is the same today, tomorrow, and yesterday, and resides outside of time, He can be invited into that past trauma to give you a new picture with Him in it.

We encourage the traumatized person to ask Jesus, "What would You have done if You had been there with me?" I have seen again and again Jesus show them a new picture with Him in it. This personal encounter with His presence in their trauma neutralizes its power and allows the person to move forward from that event and begin to live life again. Make sure they know the Lord as Savior prior to praying with them for the trauma.

Sample Prayer for Traumatized Individuals:

> *"Lord, if You had been there when this happened to me, what would You have done?*
>
> *I invite You into this memory. I allow You to enter into it and change it with Your presence.*

Allow the person time to "see" or picture Jesus walk into that specific memory. Ask them to tell you what they see Him doing to rescue them from the trauma. As they share their picture with you, ask the Lord to make it a reality to them. Ask Him to take away their pain and carry them to the safety of His presence.

8. EXCHANGING TRUTH FOR LIES

Key Scriptures

> *"Then you will know the truth, and the truth will set you free."*

John 8:32

> *Wherefore God gave them up in the lusts of their hearts unto uncleanness, that their bodies should be dishonored among themselves: for that they exchanged the truth of God for a lie, and worshipped and served the creature rather than the Creator, who is blessed forever.*

Romans 1:24-25

Truth is not what you think, nor is it what I think. It is not a precept, concept, or opinion. Truth is a Person. John 14:6 is our reference for this statement. Jesus is speaking and decrees: "I Am the Way, the Truth, and the Life..." The enemy is the father of lies, deceives us to get a stronghold in our lives. When we minister to people who are believing a lie about themselves, it is important to ask the Spirit of Truth to tell them the truth about their situation. Finding a scripture that negates the lie they are believing is key to freeing them from it. The Spirit of Truth is Holy Spirit and it is His job to keep us from delusion and deception. Years ago, I asked Him, the Spirit of Truth, to be my friend and keep me from the deceptions of false religion, watered down scripture, manipulation, and control. He has been faithful to do so.

When you perceive that the person you are trying to help is

believing lies, help them find the truth through scripture. Teach them to speak the truth to themselves out loud, because it will build their faith as they do so.

Sample Prayer to Exchange the Lie for the Truth:

> *Father in the Name of Jesus, I ask Your forgiveness for believing a lie that is contrary to the truth in your word. I chose to let go of the lie/lies I have believed and trade them in for what Your word declares over me. I ask the Spirit of Truth to be my friend and keep me from delusion, deception, and manipulation by the enemy of my soul. Thank you, Lord for showing me the truth about every situation in my life.*

Assist them in listing the lies they are believing and take them through exchanging each one for the specific truth from God's word that negates them. Then, have them choose verbally to exchange each lie for the truth.

9. ABORTION

Abortion violates one of the Ten Commandments. *"You shall not murder"* (Exodus 20:13 NIV).

It also destroys a reward sent by the Lord into your life. *"Children are a heritage from the LORD, offspring a reward from him"* (Psalm 127:3 NIV).

After speaking at a conference a few years ago, we opened up the opportunity for ministry. I was praying for those who had responded. About half way through the line, a middle-aged woman stood before me. She told me she wanted prayer for physical healing. I started to pray for her when Holy Spirit dropped the word, "abortion" in my spirit. I have learned to listen to His voice, so I asked her, "Why is the Lord giving me the word, abortion?" She looked at me with surprise and proceeded to tell me, with tears in her eyes, that she had aborted three babies.

The Lord showed me that the root of her physical problems was the sin of abortion.

I led her in a prayer of repentance for sacrificing her babies on the altar of convenience. As she genuinely allowed the Lord to cleanse her heart from the murder of her own children, the physical pain and anxiety lifted from her body and she experienced healing.

Sample prayer of repentance from abortion:

> *Father, in the name of Jesus, I ask Your forgiveness for aborting my child/children. I now know abortion is murder. I now know even if the children are conceived without the benefit of covenant, they are still Your gifts. Forgive me, Father, I release this child (these children) into Your hands. I know I will be reunited with them in eternity. I receive Your cleansing, Your forgiveness for my sin. Please allow our family line to once again be blessed with the heritage of children.*

Because abortion is so damaging to a woman's emotions, it is important to allow Holy Spirit to bring healing. Ask the Lord to release the healing balm of heaven as a salve to penetrate deep into the recesses of those damaged emotions.

10. SUICIDAL THOUGHTS

Key Scripture

> *The thief comes only to steal and kill and destroy;*
> *I have come that they may have life, and have it*
> *to the full.*

John 10:10

Just yesterday, we heard that a middle age woman we knew had killed herself. She was fighting an inner, hidden battle that no one knew about. Self-destruction is not normal behavior. In fact, it is the result of oppressive thoughts instigated by the enemy whose desire is to annihilate us.

Recently I was teaching a class on freedom, when Holy Spirit said there was someone there who was fighting the spirit of suicide. I stopped teaching and asked if anyone was fighting that spirit. Two people opened up their hearts and confessed their inner battle. One was young, the other was old. We prayed for them and commanded that lying spirit to depart. The lie is that death would deliver them from all their problems. Death is not a deliverer, Jesus is!

The power of suicide is negated as it is exposed to the light. Our enemy traffics in darkness. When these inner negative thoughts are shared with someone else, the power they hold diminishes. That spirit has to be exposed and banished. It must be commanded to leave.

Sample prayer of repentance for thoughts of suicide:

> *Father: I confess that I have believed the lies of the*
> *enemy that say I would be better off dead. I stand*
> *against such deception and receive your blessings*

for my life. I further commit to working through the issues in my life that have led me to believe this lie. I will seek out your restoration for all that afflicts me, including guilt, remorse, shame, fear, condemnation, hopelessness, and oppression. I ask and believe for your forgiveness, and confess that all my sins were dealt with by Jesus' blood shed on the cross. I accept your new life and the healing that flows from Jesus' resurrection. I am not a victim. I am a victor in Jesus Christ. Amen.

AFTERCARE

"Now the Lord is the Spirit, and where the Spirit of the Lord is, there is liberty [emancipation from bondage, true freedom]."

2 Corinthians 3:17 AMP

Freedom must be maintained. Each person must learn to develop a personal relationship with God through His Son Jesus, learning to express their need to the Lord through prayer, learning to war for themselves. By remaining in fellowship with the body of Christ, they can be discipled. Being surrounded by other Christians will keep them from being isolated from the help they need on an ongoing basis. Encourage them to read the Bible and listen to healing, uplifting worship music. Stay in contact with them as they walk the path to total restoration.

Deliverance To Freedom

Biography

Regina Shank is the author of The Standard Bearer - Wisdom From America's Heartland. In addition, she has written numerous articles, poems, and devotions for a variety of publications. Her column, The Standard Bearer, is published by The Carthage Press, in Carthage, MO.

She is the founder and President of Missouri Prayer Global Ministries (an apostolic ministry aligned with Network Ekklesia International with Apostle Dutch Sheets, Global Spheres with Chuck Pierce and Global Reformers with Robert Henderson), recently renamed Global Transformation International. She is a member of International Society of Deliverance Ministers. She also is the founder and director of Feeding Inc., a feeding outreach ministry in southwest Missouri.

Regina teaches on prayer, prophetic and strategic intercession, warfare, deliverance, and the importance of a strong personal relationship with Jesus. She has served in several leadership roles in the body of Christ, leading prayer trips to Romania, Italy, Bosnia, Ethiopia, Egypt, Israel, Hungary, Russia, and China. She and her husband, Mick, have three children and five grandchildren. Mick is a real estate appraiser and the mayor of their small community in southwest Missouri.

p. 124 *Testimony of a woman who had turned to shopping when she was overwhelmed (insted of turning to God.) He told her it was an <u>idol</u> !!

p. 125 Examples of idols today.

P. 126 Results of occult involvement
oppression, depression, religious delusions, unrelenting anxiety, self-pity destructive thoughts + actions

126 Complete list of things people get involved with.